learning ENVIRONMENTS for children

HENRY SANOFF ■ JOAN SANOFF

HUMANICS LEARNING
The Most Trusted Name in Education
Humanics Learning is an imprint of Humanics Limited

Second Printing, 1988
Copyright © 1981 Humanics Limited

PRINTED IN THE UNITED STATES OF AMERICA

Library of Congress Catalogue Card Number: 81-81659

ISBN 0-89334-065-0

ACKNOWLEDGEMENTS

The original report was developed, in part, at the School of Design, North Carolina State University at Raleigh, with the assistance of students of the Community Development Group. Special acknowledgement is due to Michael McNamara and Peter Knowland for their graphic work. Organizational assistance was provided by Anderson Hensley, Richard Busse, Jim Heffner, Richard Kattenburg, Henry White.

The project was supported, in part, by contract PLD - 2719-73 from the Center for Studies of Child and Family Mental Health. National Institute of Mental Health. Washington, D.C., 1973.

This second edition was rewritten to include a major revision in the curriculum planning aspects of children's environments. The changes were made as a result of five years of testing with architects and educators.

to
ari & zöe

contents

introduction

The emergence of early learning in America today is being advanced for two main reasons. First, psychologists such as Deutsch, in his book, *The Disadvantaged Child,* have demonstrated that a child's intelligence is not fixed at birth, but in fact, can be dramatically affected by the child's experiences and his/her environment, especially in the early ages. Secondly, the growing awareness of the influence of poverty and environmental deprivation on a child's intellectual development has given these findings an urgent practical application. These factors, coupled with the need to provide child care services for working mothers, in order that they may recognize their self worth, have placed a major responsibility upon local communities to integrate early childhood education with day care.

The objective of this report is to furnish guidelines for creating learning environments for children centers. It can be used for the creation of new centers, re-design of existing centers or when remodelling existing buildings.

The intent is to stress the interrelatedness of the goals of childrens developmental programs and the physical environment in which they are housed.

In order to clearly present design guidelines, each of the activity areas that might be contained in a center are described in terms of their objectives, design requirements, participants and the molecular activities engaged in by children. The objectives attempt to clarify the way in which the activities support and nurture the child's development. The design requirements merely state relationships for the appropriate functioning of the activity area. Various educational approaches, whether emphasizing free choice or highly structured programs, can be accommodated by the way in which the activity areas are organized. The molecular activities describe what the expected range of behaviors might be in the activity areas.

Diagrams are used to illustrate, but not determine, the way in which the activity areas should be organized. The organizational diagrams, however, only suggest relationships between the participants and aspects of the physical environment.

Differing community needs, programs and objectives should serve as criteria which will modify the way in which these guidelines are employed.

CREATING AN ENVIRONMENT

goals

The intent of this planning process is to furnish guidelines that stress the inter-relatedness between children's developmental goals and the environment that accommodates them. This sequential process proposes to facilitate the making of children's places more responsive to their learning.

The recognition of children's needs and learning processes is a prerequisite to the formulation of goals for a child development program. These goals are first defined in terms of the major areas of learning and growth that are regarded to be crucial. Second, these goals can be adapted to provide a stimulating environment that encourages children to respond to and to develop their specific needs and capacities.

The children's center, school and home share in the child's development in all stages of his or her growth. Corresponding to the general needs of young children, the goals of a center should:

Bring competence in the physical-motor, social-emotional and intellectual skills;
Encourage creative expression and invention;
Nurture individuality in ways that contribute to feelings of worth and self-identity.

These goals need to correspond to the different developmental stages of children. It is in the enhancement of the developmental process that educational goals can contribute towards programmatic growth.

Goals are generalized statements about the overall purpose of the program. Goals initiate and generate the experiences children can engage in and include the major areas of learning and growth.

Formulate the goals within the following areas of development:

Social Development

To advance and develop the child's functioning knowledge of his/her environment

Individual Development

_____

_____

_____

Intellectual Development

EXAMPLE

_____

_____

_____

Include factors within the classroom environment that would enhance the goals you have stated.

observations of the community through visitation and demonstration story reading and role playing about work processes, peoples roles and functions

Develop a set of goals for an educational program in developmental terms. Include those factors in the classroom that foster these goals.

Formulate the goals within the following areas of development:

Social Development

_____

_____

_____

Individual Development

_____

_____

_____

Intellectual Development

_____

_____

_____

Include factors within the classroom environment that would enhance the goals you have stated.

_____

_____

_____

_____

The following set of goals are stated in developmental terms to include factors within the environment that foster the goals.

Social Development

To help the child develop controls for appropriate handling of drives and internalize impulse control and conflicts.

The school environment should provide for:

Communicating a clear set of non-threatening controls, such as limits, rules and regulations.

Creating a functional adult authority role which sets understandable restraints, non-punitive sanctions and alternative behavior patterns.

Fostering special relations of child to adult and guidance in learning to share things as well as people.

To advance and develop the child's functioning knowledge of his/her environment.

The school environment should provide for:

Observation of the community environment through visitation and demonstration.

Story reading about work processes, people's roles and functions.

Discussion of contemporary events which children hear discussed, such as war, demonstrations, outer-space activities.

To provide a positive emotional climate in which the child learns to trust others and himself/herself.

The school environment should provide for:

Building informal communication channels, verbal and non-verbal, which include adult-to-child and child-to-child.

Cooperative and collective child/group discussion periods and joint work projects.

Creating supportive adult role where the adult is a source of comfort, trouble-shooter and has an investment in the child's learning.

Individual Development

To facilitate the development of an image of self, as a unique competent person.

The school environment should provide for:

An increasing knowledge of self, through identity, family ethnic membership and awareness of skills.

Constructive, manipulative activities with a variety of materials, such as sand, clay and wood.

Intellectual Development

To promote the potential for ordering experience through cognitive strategies.

The school environment should provide for:

Developing and extending receptiveness by a variety of sensory-motor-perceptual experiences that focus on observational discrimination.

Extending modes of symbolizing through gestural representation, two dimensional representation and three dimensional exercises.

Developing facility with language through word meanings and usage, scope of vocabulary, meaningful verbal communication and expression and mastery of syntax.

Development of stimulating verbal-conceptual organization of experience and problem solving skills through accent on classification, ordering, relationship and transformational concepts in a varied experimental context and through selective play materials.

To support the play mode of incorporating experience.

The school environment should provide for:

An atmosphere that nourishes and sets the stage for dramatic play activity by providing experiences, materials and props.

Freedom to go beyond the restraints of reality in representing experiences.

For a further discussion of developmental goals refer to *Promoting Cognitive Growth* by Biber, Shapiro and Wickens.

activity areas

Now that you have formulated a set of goals within the given constraints, it is necessary to organize those general statements into learning objectives.

Learning objectives are statements that describe the desired characteristics to be achieved by each child. These statements can provide the stimulus for planning children's experiences.

Using the example described in the goal section:

Social Development

To advance and develop the child's functioning knowledge of his/her environment.

the following learning objectives were generated:

positive self image
language development

Develop a set of learning objectives appropriate to your goals.

The objectives that have been formulated attempt to clarify the way in which activity areas can support and nurture a child's development.

Educational program approaches that emphasize free choice or structure can easily accommodate the organization of activity areas.

An activity area is a section of the learning environment described by specific materials and physical boundaries. They are specific places where learning experiences occur. The environment is subdivided into areas to order the room, limit chaos and encourage children to pursue planned activities.

The activity areas selected for a classroom should be selected on the basis of teaching style, the known and anticipated needs of the children and the physical space of the classroom. The basic arrangement of a learning environment is significant in the type of activity that is generated. The three major areas of stimulation to be considered in designing the activity areas are:

Sensory stimulation excites the senses. Activity areas should be colorful and contain appropriate visual material generally relevant to that area. Sensory stimulation is enhanced by diversity in the environment through patterns, textures, objects, shapes and forms, where children have the opportunity to touch, to smell, to listen and to taste a variety of materials.

Activity stimulation comes from spatial arrangements that encourage children to participate in activities while defining the scope and limitations of the activities.

Cognitive stimulation refers to the teacher's utilization of the environment to encourage children to work in areas and at levels that will promote their intellectual development.

Using the learning objectives derived from the goal example, specific activity areas are illustrated below which satisfy those objectives.

Positive Self-Image

art
dramatic play
blocks

Language Development

reading
writing
dramatic play

Role Enactment

dramatic play
blocks

Develop a set of activity areas appropriate to to your learning objectives.

_____

_____

_____

_____

_____

_____

_____

_____

_____

_____

In order to identify how certain learning objectives can be fulfilled in the various activity centers, an illustration comparing information categories is shown on the right. An example of such a display is called a matrix, where a check mark is placed in the grid corresponding to the appropriate pair of relationships. Similarly, a good way to describe what happens in activity centers is to make a display showing the secondary activities that occur in each center.

Diagram showing comparisons between activity areas and learning objectives.

LEARNING OBJECTIVES	ACTIVITY CENTERS																			
	cubby/locker	large group	listening	water play	sand	dramatic play	art	blocks	manipulative	science	reading	writing	construction	indoor active	math	concept formation	music	movement	cooking	visual aids	protected outdoor
positive self-image																				
skill development																				
problem solving																				
experimentation																				
concept formation																				
sensory & perceptual acuity																				
eye hand coordination																				
large/small muscle development																				
visual discrimination																				
language development																				
oral																				
recognition of symbols																				
individual functioning in groups																				
self expression																				
role enactment-fantisizing																				
observing																				
socializing																				
sensory awareness																				
self-esteem																				
selfknowledge																				
exploration																				
planning																				

planning

Children's behavior in the activity centers can be described as secondary activities. The activity center acts as a stimulus to generate the activities that occur. The life of the activity center is in the learning materials and the activities these materials facilitate.

Given the freedom to learn, the innate inquisitiveness and fascination with the world they possess, children learn for and by themselves, or with each other's help through the materials in the activity centers. A child can choose his or her own learning activities and build confidence by so doing. There should be options in the environment for different learning styles from which children can derive positive feelings and self-confidence.

To illustrate the use of secondary activities, the original example of the *art* activity center will be examined. The following are secondary activities that could occur within the *art* center.

Secondary Activities

pasting
cutting
drawing
painting
washing
modeling

Develop a set of secondary activities for each activity center that is relevant to your classroom.

_____
_____
_____
_____
_____
_____
_____
_____
_____
_____
_____
_____
_____
_____
_____
_____
_____
_____
_____
_____
_____

SECONDARY ACTIVITIES	ACTIVITY CENTERS

Columns (SECONDARY ACTIVITIES): arranging, balancing, weighing, mixing, modeling, creating, dramatizing, tasting, feeling, classifying, ordering, stacking, experimenting, measuring, writing, dictating

Rows (ACTIVITY CENTERS): cubby/locker, large group, listening, water play, sand, dramatic play, art, blocks, manipulative, science, reading, writing, construction, indoor active, math, concept formation, music, movement, cooking, visual aids, protected outdoor

Diagram showing comparisons between activity centers and secondary activities.

Now that activity centers and relevant secondary activities have been identified, it is necessary to select materials appropriate to the secondary activities that will facilitate learning experiences for the *art* center.

Secondary Activities	Materials
pasting	paste
	paper
cutting	scissors
	paper
drawing	crayons
	paper
painting	brushes
	paint
washing	water
	playdough
modeling	clay
	water

List the materials appropriate to the activity centers and secondary activities you have selected.

_____

_____

_____

_____

_____

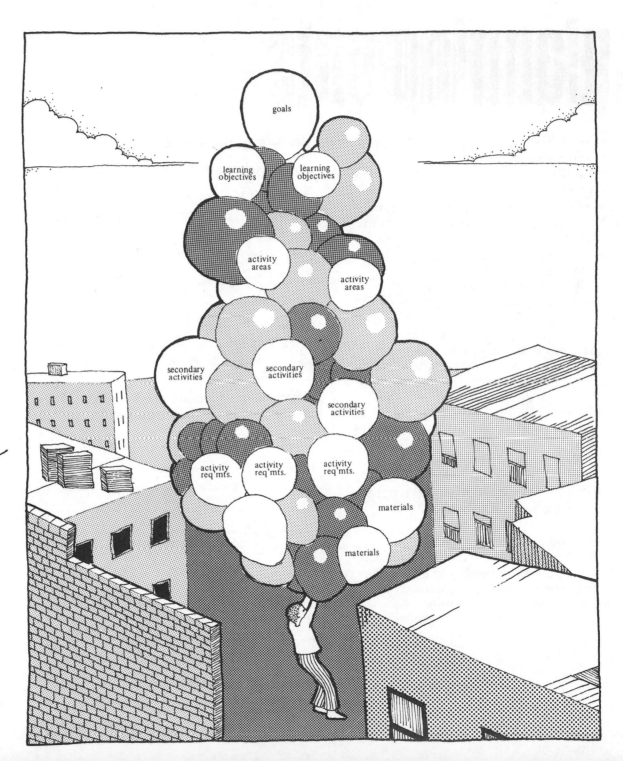

requirements

The art work of children is a visual expression of their feelings about experiences that are personally significant to them. The feelings they choose to express can result from direct involvement in home or school activities or from vicarious experiences in listening to stories and in reading. In order to express their thoughts visually, children must think about themselves and their socio-physical environment. For this reason, art activities are valuable for intellectual development and for self-image formation. Art can mean invention to children and thus it becomes important for self-expression, communication and problem solving. Working individually, while controlling their actions, children learn technical skills, gain self-reliance and achieve positive self-images. Variety in art activities is limited only by the teacher's choice of materials to make available for the children's use. An *art* center should be usable by both individuals and groups without significant interference.

Learning objectives, secondary activities and materials have been identified for the art area. It is now necessary to define the activity requirements to accommodate the desired secondary activities.

Activity Requirements-ART

provide for individual & group
activities
provide vertical & horizontal
work surfaces
provide storage for
incomplete projects
provide space for
drying art work
provide storage accessible
to children

Develop a list of requirements for each of the activity centers you have selected.

The location of an activity center should be considered with respect to the necessary relations to other centers. The criteria used for establishing the spatial relationships that are extremely important are traffic between centers and other environmental disturbances such as noise.

List the activities in your center/classroom that are either noisy or quiet.

Quiet   **Noisy**

———————— ————————

———————— ————————

———————— ————————

———————— ————————

———————— ————————

Connect those activities that have the greatest amount of frequency of movement between them.

Are the quiet activities adjacent to each other?

Is there excessive movement between quiet activities?

Are your activities occurring in the appropriate areas?

Are there any changes that would be beneficial?

Does your classroom arrangement allow children to be involved without imposing on the rights of other children?

The tasks that have been completed in the process of creating an environment for children are basic to structuring relevant learning experiences.

Planning is necessary to utilize the environment to encourage children to work at their own rate and level in an area of their own choosing.

Planning the environment can help to provide the experiences in a child's preferred sensory mode of learning, such as touch, sight, hearing, smell, taste or movement.

The organization of classroom space can encourage children to participate in activities and aid them in defining their scope and limitations.

Planning can provide options to a child for pursuing a particular interest in a manner best suited to learning.

It is now necessary to develop the learning objectives into performance objectives. This stage of the process requires that statements be developed that pertain to specific activities and behaviors. The task for this exercise will require that you specify the objectives for one day or week, in order to plan specific activities for each center.

Select one major learning objective.

develop senses and perception

Develop a performance statement from the learning objective. Consider an objective that may be achieved in one day.

develop a sense of touch (child feels hot-cold, rough-smooth.)

Examine each activity center and identify the secondary activities that will promote your daily objective. Plan for specific activities to occur at each center.

Large group - introduce touching words
Art - collage of geometric shapes and volumes
Science - use thermometer to measure water temperature
Concept formation - display rough and smooth objects for manipulation
Language - read how things feel

Select one major learning objective.

Develop a performance statement from the learning objective. Consider an objective that may be achieved in one day.

Examine each activity center and identify the secondary activities that will promote your daily objective. Plan for specific activities to occur at each center.

evaluation

How do we evaluate our accomplishments?

Evaluation can be described as the process of regularly determining if the learning objectives are being realized, and if they are stimulating appropriate changes.

The evaluation process requires:

Identification of learning objectives and their appropriate activity centers.

Selection of materials or equipment necessary to achieve the learning objectives;

Coordination of home and school learning objectives, lifestyles and expectations.

The classroom environment should be designed to respond to the learners. A major learning objective is to nurture self-directed, self-regulated children. When observing children's behavior, it is necessary to be aware of the wide range of variations that can occur. Playing and working are activities that children engage in through specific learning situations. The child's developmental level, mood, personality, in addition to the materials available, all have an influence on observable behavior.

In order to efficiently observe and accurately evaluate the child's performance, it is necessary to utilize techniques that will help to systematize the recording of children's behavior.

Included in this part of the process are examples of recording forms that focus on the environmental characteristics that are related to the individual child's assessment.

Teachers task:	*Observe and evaluate specific learning objectives to determine if the objectives bring about desired changes.*
Specific objective:	*Child feels a variety of textures and describes them verbally.*
Child's name:	————————
Date:	————————
Time:	from———— to————
Activity center:	*Art Center - concept formation*
Materials:	————————
Children involved:	————————
How initiated?	————————
What was said?	————————
By whom?	————————
Evaluate:	*Was the objective achieved? How can this information be used for further planning?*

TEACHER'S TASK: Observe and evaluate specific learning objectives to determine if the objectives bring about desired changes.

OBJECTIVE: The child feels a variety of textures and describes them verbally.

Child's Name _____ Date_____ Time _____

ACTIVITY CENTER: Art Center - Concept Formation

Materials Used _____ Objects Used _____

Participants _____

ACTION PATTERN RATINGS										
SUPERVISION		STRUCTURE		VERBAL			TEMPO			
supervise	unsuper.	organized	unorgan.	loud	med.	soft	fast	med.	slow	

BEHAVIORAL MECHANISM RATINGS														
GROSS MOTOR			MANIP.			VERBAL			AFFECTIVE			THINKING		
H	M	L	H	M	L	H	M	L	H	M	L	H	M	L

Listed below are a series of questions that can provide a basis for observations. Use them as a guide to what you might do.

Which children come to your mind first? Why?

Which children seem comfortable in the learning environment?

Which children have difficulty adjusting to:
   classroom routines,
   rules and limits,
   the activities where difficulty occurred.

Which children seem overly active? When? What activities?

Which children seem overly withdrawn or non-verbal?
   Continue observation based on child's stages of play from solitary, parallel and peer play.
   Observe the use of language at home, in the neighborhood, and at school.
   Is the language at home different from the teacher's?

What activity centers did children use and enjoy most?

Which activity centers were not used?

Where would be the best place to set up the reading area?

Why is the art center always so messy?

Why is there excessive running and unwanted movement in the room?

ACTIVITY ANALYSIS

This section describes techniques for relating objectives for learning to children's activities in their appropriate environmental setting. The procedures can be used by small groups or by individuals.

Any recognized activity or unit of activity should be considered in respect to the necessary relations between other activities and to basic physical requirements. Activities and activity sets or systems are so closely related to our understanding of the physical facilities which conditions them that we sometimes describe an activity in terms of the type of physical "place" or facility in which it is performed without fully understanding the relationship.

In order to realize the relation between the organization and employment of physical elements in space and the human activities which determine their employment, an independent view of the activity itself was conducted, free of any preconceived spatial attitudes. Therefore, the activity analysis is essentially a study of the boundary conditions of the system and the enveloping environment.

A graphic method was selected for describing the basic relationships. A simple coding system was used to suggest qualitative differences between activities so that a wide array of alternative relationships would be possible.

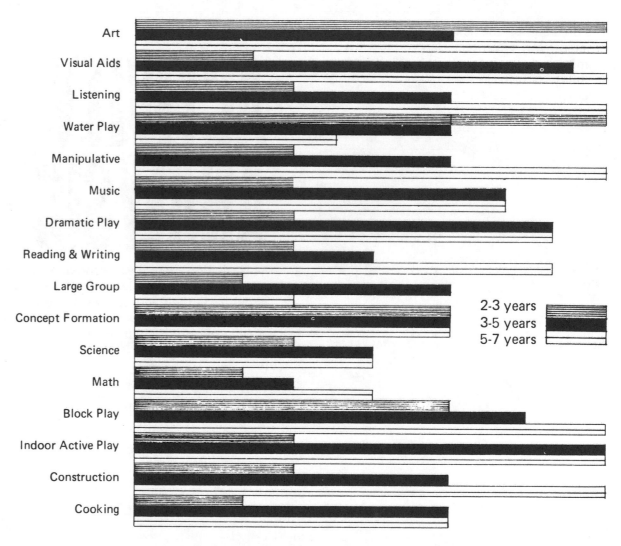

Comparison between activity center usage by age groups.

The drawings on the next page depict different activity centers. Can you identify them? Are there certain materials, objects or children's behaviors that suggest a specific activity center?

a————————— b—————————
c————————— d—————————
e————————— f—————————
g————————— h—————————
i————————— j—————————
k————————— l—————————

Each of the activity centers can be described using the adjective pairs on this page. Select one adjective from each set to rate the following activity centers.

Activity Center (c)	Activity Center (e)
- - - - - - - - - - - -	- - - - - - - - - - - -
——————————	——————————
——————————	——————————
——————————	——————————
——————————	——————————
——————————	——————————
——————————	——————————
——————————	——————————
——————————	——————————
——————————	——————————
——————————	——————————
——————————	——————————
——————————	——————————

restricted space	free space
obscure	clear
single-purpose	multi-purpose
unpleasant	pleasant
unfinished	finished
common	unique
unimaginative	imaginative
boring	interesting
happy	sad
unfriendly	friendly
ordinary	distinctive
simple	complex
usual	unusual
old fashioned	modern

THE PROCESS OF CREATING A LEARNING ENVIRONMENT

settings

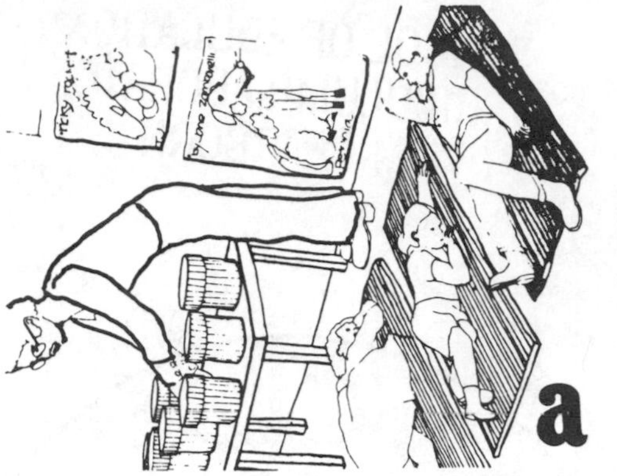

a

b

c

d

e

f

g

h

i

j

k

l

group decision making

Planning Environments for Children is a method of facilitating the process for planning meaningful places for children.

The interactional game process consists of three stages, each of which requires a set of cards. You will need to supply your own cards using the catagories described below. Cards should be prepared prior to the time at which you plan to begin.

To make the cards, cut colored construction paper into strips of one inch by four inches. You will require 23 strips of one color for the *ACTIVITIES* and 36 strips of another color for the *OBJECTIVES.*

OBJECTIVES: The purpose of learning.

ACTIVITIES: The things children do in the environment.

SETTINGS: Places where children can perform the activities. (Xerox the illustrations)

This structured experience is to be used by a group of three to five people, although many groups may participate at the same time. To begin, each person selects, from the list provided, no more than five *OBJECTIVES* which seem to be most important. Brief notes should be made justifying each choice. After each person has made his/her choices, individual lists are pooled, and the corresponding *OBJECTIVE* cards are pulled from the deck.

OBJECTIVE cards are arranged, face up, so they can be seen by all. Through collaboration, the group must choose from these no more than five cards which should be able to be incorporated into a single, unified educational program. Players are urged to forcefully support their individual choices. Continue discussions until consensus is reached on the five *OBJECTIVES* your group feels are most important. Since this may require a considerable amount of time, discussions can be limited to 30 minutes. After completing this phase, group members should record their final choices on the record sheet.

Next, as a group, examine each *OBJECTIVE* individually, and select three *ACTIVITIES* that can be used to accomplish each *OBJECTIVE.* (You should work through each *OBJECTIVE* completely before starting a new one.) Keep in mind that some *ACTIVITIES* may be used with more than one *OBJECTIVE.*

Then, combining *OBJECTIVES* and *ACTIVITIES,* choose a physical *SETTING* that can be used to fulfill the requirements of each *OBJECTIVE.* Remember, *SETTINGS* should provide the right kind of props, materials and equipment to allow for the successful performance of the *ACTIVITIES* on your record sheet.

RECORD SHEET

Objectives   Activities   Setting

1

2

3

4

5

activities

objectives

ART
MANIPULATIVES
WATER PLAY
MEASURING
CONSTRUCTION
ANIMAL CARE
CUBBIES
TABLE GAMES
ROLE PLAY
PLANT CARE
WEIGHING
LISTENING
READING
MUSIC
BLOCK PLAY
EATING
OUTDOOR ACTIVE PLAY
COOKING
SCIENCE
GROUP GAMES
SAND PLAY
RESTING

Developing Language Fluency
Encouraging Student's Sense of Community Identity
Reinforcing Sense of Effectiveness of the Individual
Developing Cognitive Skills
Developing Motivation for Learning
Encouraging Self-Expression
Reinforcing Positive Self-Image
Developing a Sense of Confidence
Developing Persistence Toward A Goal
Developing Concentration
Developing Self-Regulation
Learning by Discrimination
Developing Communication Skills
Developing Concept Formation
Channeling Basic Biological Drives Constructively
Developing/Encouraging Resourcefulness
Developing Initiative and Spontaneity
Developing Introspective Skills
Developing Social Competence
Developing Tolerance of Differences
Developing A Sense of Responsibility
Learning by Conditioning
Encouraging Group Interaction
Learning Through Execution
Stimulating Curiosity and Imagination
Developing A Sense of Reality
Achieving Intra-Sensory Integration
Developing Motor Skills
Learning by Example
Developing Memory Skills
Developing Self-Actualization
Encouraging A Sense of Trust
Constructive Use of Fantasy
Developing Perceptual Acuity
Involving Parents In The Educational Experience
Developing Social Awareness

INTER-RELATIONSHIPS BETWEEN CHILDRENS ACTIVITIES
BASED ON PROXIMITY AND COMPATABILITY OF ACTIVITIES

	ART	VISUAL AIDS	LISTENING	WATER	MANIPULATIVE	MUSIC	DRAMA	READING	LARGE GROUP	CONCEPT FORMATION	SCIENCE	MATH	BLOCKS	INDOOR ACTIVE	CONSTRUCTION	NAPPING	CUBBY	LOCKERS	EATING	COOKING	TOILET	WASHING	ENTRY
ART																							
VISUAL AIDS	L																						
LISTENING	M	H																					
WATER	H	L	L																				
MANIPULATIVE	M	M	H	L																			
MUSIC	L	L	L	L	L																		
DRAMA	L	M	L	L	L	H																	
READING	L	H	H	L	H	L	L																
LARGE GROUP	L	H	H	L	L	H	M	L															
CONCEPT FORMATION	L	M	H	L	H	M	L	H	H														
SCIENCE	M	M	M	H	L	L	L	H	L	H													
MATH	L	M	L	M	H	L	L	H	L	H	H												
BLOCKS	L	L	L	L	L	M	M	L	L	L	L	M											
INDOOR ACTIVE	L	L	L	L	L	M	M	H	L	M	L	L	H										
CONSTRUCTION	L	L	L	L	L	L	L	L	L	M	M	M	H	H									
NAPPING	L	L	M	L	M	H	L	L	H	L	L	L	L	L	L								
CUBBY	M	M	M	L	L	H	L	M	L	L	L	L	L	L	L	H							
LOCKERS	L	L	L	L	M	L	M	L	M	L	L	L	L	L	L	L	M						
EATING	L	L	M	M	L	L	L	L	M	L	L	L	L	L	L	L	H	L					
COOKING	H	L	L	H	L	L	L	L	L	L	M	L	L	L	L	L	L	L	H				
TOILET	M	L	M	M	L	L	L	L	L	L	L	L	L	L	M	L	H	H	H	M			
WASHING	H	L	L	H	L	M	M	L	L	L	L	M	L	L	L	H	H	H	H	H	H		
ENTRY	L	L	L	L	M	L	L	L	L	M	L	L	L	L	L	L	H	H	L	L	M	M	

INTERACTION SCALE
L=LOW
M=MEDIUM
H=HIGH

space planning

The graphic symbols represent activities that are common to all children's centers. The symbols include the administrative services of a center (director, staff, etc.), the children's indoor activities (art, manipulative, etc.) and the children's outdoor activities (climbing, swinging, etc.).

In order to use the graphic symbols for the purpose of planning a children's center or a classroom, draw a one inch by one inch grid on a sheet of paper. A 9 inch by 12 inch sheet size should be adequate to lay out the activities contained in a classroom.

The rules for arranging the activity symbols on the grid board are as follows:

Each activity symbol should be placed on vacant grid.

No two symbols should overlap or occupy more than one grid cell.

Relationships can be planned between activities such that some may be adjacent to each other while others may require some separation.

Each activity symbol can have direct contact with four other activities. This suggests that the placement of activities on the grid will require decisions about the most important relationships.

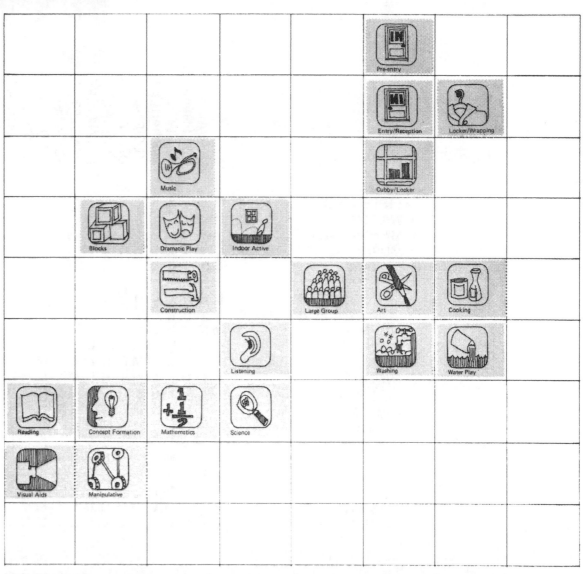

This illustration represents one alternative generated by a group of three teachers. This spatial planning process can be conducted with small groups or experienced individually.

activity diagrams

Health	Locker/Wrapping	Cubby/Locker
Observation	Large Group	Toilet
Director		
Washing	Kitchen	Eating
Sleeping	Visual Aids	Listening
Entry/Reception		
Water Play	Dramatic Play	Art
Blocks	Manipulative	Science
Staff/Lounge		
Reading	Construction	Sand
Climbing	Swinging	Open
Parent/Community		
Concept Formation	Mathematics	Indoor Active
Music	Cooking	Protected Outdoor
Laundry		

DESIGN A CHILDRENS CENTER

PROGRAM

This section contains descriptions of each of the activity areas found in a children's center. Each activity center is described verbally and graphically. A notation system was developed in order to describe relationships between the qualities of *surfaces, screens and objects.* These components represent the physical parts that help to shape the activity center. Diagrams are also used to describe the secondary activities occurring in the center. The graphic notation system is a diagrammatic aid to be used in conjunction with the design requirements, to further describe the unique characteristics of each activity center.

The contents of this part of the book are often referred to as a *program.*

graphic symbols

Sitting Apparatus	Resting Apparatus	Climbing Apparatus	Swinging Apparatus	Cooking Apparatus
Parking	Stationary Storage	Records Storage	Portable Storage	Musical Instruments
Vertical Work Surface	Horizontal Work Surface	Mirror Surface	Weather Protection	Potential Darkness
Telephone	Visual Aids	Dramatic Props	Science Materials	Reading Material
Audio Aids	Manipulative Toys	Art Tools	Art Supplies	Food Preparation Equipment
Art Drying Apparatus	Animals	Television	Typewriter	Food
Clothes Storage	Sand	Vegetation	Math Materials	Refreshments
Water Play Props	Construction Tools	Napping Pads	Blocks & Props	Clothes Washing Equipment
Drinking Water	Sink	Toilet	Garbage	Refrigeration Equipment

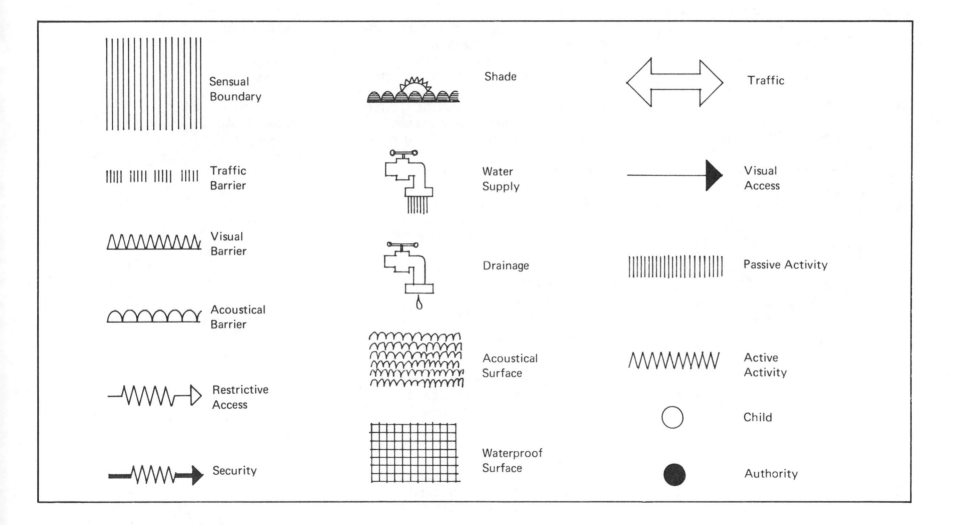

Sensual Boundary

Traffic Barrier

Visual Barrier

Acoustical Barrier

Restrictive Access

Security

Shade

Water Supply

Drainage

Acoustical Surface

Waterproof Surface

Traffic

Visual Access

Passive Activity

Active Activity

Child

Authority

pre entry

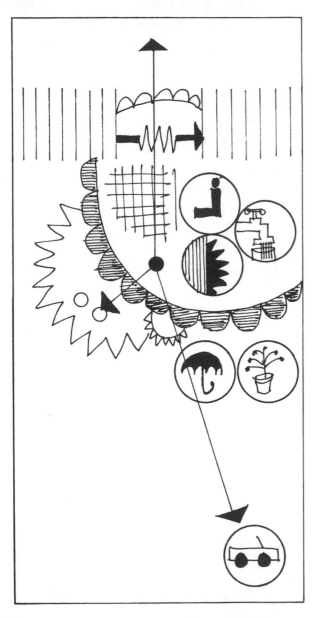

The pre-entry is an outdoor area associated with entering and leaving the child development center. It serves as an effective environmental transition between the community and the center. The setting for this transition is especially important in dispelling the fears of children who are coming to the center for the first time. Being able to look over the building exterior and inside to the play areas is reassuring to children. The pre-entry also serves a socializing function exemplified by the tendency of families and visitors to gather in the area when weather permits outdoor activities.

Design Requirements:
1. Provide a play space for children in the pre-entry.
2. Provide both adult sized and child sized seating in the area.
3. Provide a bulletin board for community use in the area.
4. Provide adequate parking for staff, parents, and visitors near the pre-entry.
5. Provide for partial protection from the weather, particularly sun and wind.
6. Provide a variety of planting and textures in the pre-entry.
7. Provide an atmosphere in the area that is quieter than its surroundings.
8. Provide a view into the center from the pre-entry.
9. Provide the physical features that identify the pre-entry of the center to all visitors.

Participants:
children
families
visitors
staff

Molecular Activities:
relaxing
visiting
playing
entering
leaving
conversation
waiting
posting notices

entry reception

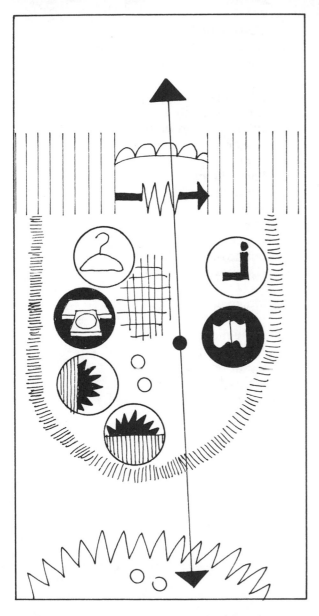

A space for entering and leaving, the entry-reception area functions primarily as an environmental transition between the outside and the inside of the child development center. In social terms, the area is a setting for welcoming people to the center and introducing them to its various aspects. It also is desirable for the qualities of the area to reassure children who are new to the center. Displaying children's art work and providing views into play areas are two ways of serving this function.

Design Requirements:
1. Provide for interaction between the receptionist and those being received.
2. Provide comfortable furniture both for adults and for children.
3. Provide horizontal work surfaces in the area for the receptionist.
4. Provide reading and displays concerning child development in the area.
5. Provide display surfaces for children's work.
6. Provide space for hanging visitor's wraps.
7. Provide a public telephone in the entry-reception area.
8. Provide flooring in the area that is durable and easily cleanable.
9. Provide views into the play areas from the entry-reception area.
10. Provide a view to the outside from the reception area.

Objectives:
welcoming
orientation
environmental transition

Participants:
children
families
visitors
staff

Molecular Activities:
entering/leaving
greeting
mingling
wrapping/unwrapping
directing
talking
waiting
displaying children's work
observing displays
secretarial work
telephoning
providing information

director

A director is a desirable part of the child development center. Usually his/her duties have two different orientations, one toward the external affairs of the center and the other toward its internal concerns. Externally, a director acts as a liason between the center and its surrounding community. For example, she is important for meeting with parents and visitors from the community and providing them with information about the center, its programs and policies. He/she also discusses children's individual problems with their parents. A director's internal duty orientation includes record keeping, supervision of clerical work, and leading teacher conferences for program planning and evaluation. An environment for a director's activities requires quietness, privacy, and enough space to accomodate groups of people and office equipment.

Design Requirements:
1. Provide for auditory and visual privacy in the director's area.
2. Provide ample horizontal work surfaces in the area.
3. Provide comfortable and movable seating for adults.
4. Provide facilities for group meetings in the area.
5. Provide storage in the area for the staff's personal possessions and for materials and equipment used by the staff.
6. Provide a telephone in the area.
7. Provide views to the outside in the director's area.

Objectives:
personal consultation
staff participation and involvement
problem solving
personnel direction
document handling
program coordination
independence

Participants:
children
visitors
families
teachers
director
clerical personnel

Molecular Activities:
interviewing
using records
telephoning
dictation
counseling
typing
filing
bookkeeping
meeting
special testing

staff

A staff area is a desirable part of the child development center. Teachers and other staff members occasionally like to take breaks from their routine responsibilities. As a place for relaxation, such an area provides visual and acoustic privacy from the clamor of children's activities. Here staff members can socialize or rest for a short time without significant interference. Teachers also need spaces where they can work independently or in planning groups. These activities can easily occur in the area if a conference table is provided. A small library also can be an important addition to a staff area.

Design Requirements:
1. Provide visual and acoustic privacy in the staff area.
2. Provide furniture that encourages informal lounging and resting in the area.
3. Provide work surfaces for individual staff members.
4. Provide seating and a table for planning and evaluation among the staff members.
5. Provide facilities for coffee service in the staff area.
6. Provide a sink in the area.
7. Provide lockable storage near the area for the staff's personal possessions.
8. Provide a telephone in the staff area.
9. Provide chalkboards and bulletin boards in the staff area.
10. Provide library facilities in the area.
11. Provide a view to the outside.
12. Provide easy access to adult toilets.

Objectives:
socialization   planning
highly concentrated activity
independence

Participants:
teacher
teacher assistants
director
clerical personnel
visitors

Molecular Activities:
meeting
coffee breaks
resting
socializing
smoking
snacking
reading
writing
telephoning

health

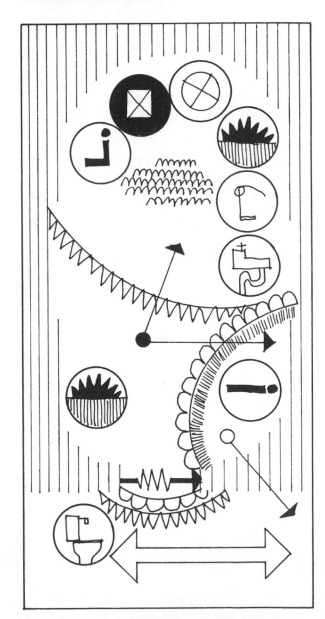

Children must be healthy before they can engage meaningfully in any learning activities in a child development center. It is probable that children who are ill and yet who go untreated will worsen their illnesses and infect others. For this reason, it is necessary that each center have some facilities for treating and isolating sick children until they can be taken home for treatment. A health facility can easily serve a secondary function as a setting for training parents in techniques of health and first aid. Probably the most important qualities of a health area are privacy for the people using it and a relaxing atmosphere. Children confined to a health area must have visual contact with other children in the center so that they do not feel isolated.

Design Requirements:
1. Provide for treatment and isolation in the health area.
2. Provide privacy in the health area.
3. Provide a bed or cot in the isolation area.
4. Provide a relaxing, homelike atmosphere in the health area with diversions for children in isolation.
5. Provide writing surfaces in the health area.
6. Provide adequate storage for examination and treatment equipment.
7. Provide a sink for children and adults in the health area.
8. Provide toilets for children near the health area.
9. Provide views to both indoor and outdoor play areas for children in isolation.
10. Provide lighting in the health area that shows accurate skin color.
11. Provide for adult supervision of the health area.
12. Provide separation between the health area and the other activity areas to prevent mutual interference.

Objectives:
health maintenance
acquisition of information
first aid training

Participants:
children
mothers
visitors
staff

Molecular Activities:
nursing	reading
observing	medicating
administering first aid	sleeping
first aid instruction	dressing/undressing
examining	keeping records
lying down	health screening
toileting	

kitchen

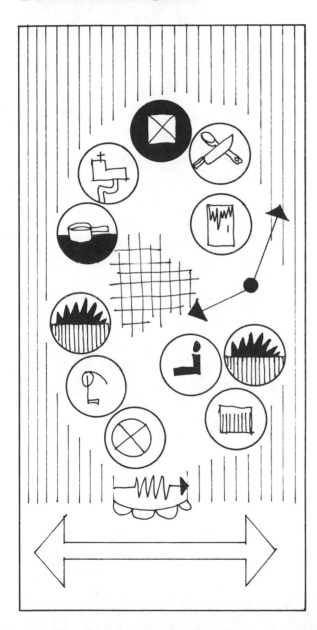

Often it is necessary for the child development center to provide complete meals for children. This service is offered particularly if the children remain at the center for long periods of time. For this reason, facilities for the preparation of large quantities of food by a trained kitchen staff may be desirable. Activities that occur in a kitchen include not only food preparation, but also storing supplies and receiving food deliveries. The kitchen environment must allow efficiency in food preparation tasks. Because kitchen activities can be somewhat dangerous, the area must be separated from the play environment and inaccessible to unsupervised children.

Design Requirements:
1. Provide both hot and cold food preparation equipment in the kitchen.
2. Provide facilities for dish washing and drying.
3. Provide facilities for waste disposal.
4. Provide for staff record keeping.
5. Provide waterproof and easily cleanable working surfaces in the area.
6. Provide ample storage for dishes, other utensils, and kitchen equipment.
7. Provide ample space for bulk storage in the kitchen which is easily accessible to service and delivery workers.
8. Provide ramps at openings to the outside for food delivery by wheeled equipment.
9. Provide separation between the kitchen and the children's domain so that activities in the two areas cannot interfere with one another.
10. Provide ventilation for the kitchen.
11. Provide views to the outside in the kitchen area.

Participants:
kitchen staff
teacher
teacher assistant
delivery and service workers

Molecular Activities:
meal planning
cooking
serving
record keeping
storing supplies and equipment
delivering supplies
washing/drying dishes
cleaning
waste disposal

parent community

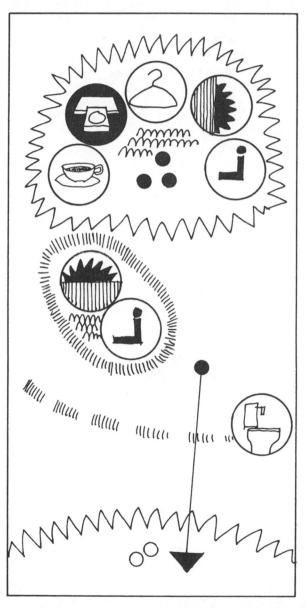

When parents bring their children to the child development center, they become participants in it. Perhaps their major activities are socializing with other parents and learning from the teachers about the needs and progress of their children. These activities suggest that a community oriented area be included in the center. In such an area, teachers and parents can confer without interfering with the children's activities. The area can function secondarily to accomodate special community activities, especially meetings. An important effect of a parent-community area is bonding the center, home and community together in a stronger relationship.

Design Requirements:

1. Provide for socializing activities in the parent-community area.
2. Provide for group meetings and private conferences in the area.
3. Provide that the area be obvious to parents as being for their use.
4. Provide information about child development in the area for the parents' use.
5. Provide display surfaces for children's work and items of community interest.
6. Provide comfortable and movable furniture for adults in the parent-community area.
7. Provide a public telephone in the area.
8. Provide easy access to adult toilets.
9. Provide views to the outside.
10. Provide separation between the parent-community area and other activities in the center to prevent mutual interference.

Objectives:
communication between parents and teachers
socialization
acquisition of information

Participants:
families
visitors
staff

Molecular Activities:
chatting
relaxing
sitting
meeting
smoking
reading
looking at displays
waiting
telephoning

SCHOOL OF EDUCATION
CURRICULUM LABORATORY
UM-DEARBORN

laundry

Occasionally, children have accidents that soil their bodies and clothing. Also, they often get excessively dirty during active outdoor play. Facilities for cleaning children and for washing and drying their clothing, therefore, are a desirable part of the child development center. Privacy for the children and ease with which the staff can perform cleaning tasks are important considerations in a laundry area.

Design Requirements:
1. Provide facilities for washing and drying clothing in the laundry area.
2. Provide a facility for washing and drying the entire child that is raised to an adult's working level.
3. Provide easily accessible storage for towels and clean clothing.
4. Provide storage for dirty clothing and laundry materials.
5. Provide surfaces in the laundry area that are waterproof and easily cleanable.
6. Provide for the minimization of drafts in the area.
7. Provide protection from circulation and other activities.

Participants:
children
teaching staff

Molecular Activities:
changing clothes
washing/drying entire child
washing/drying clothing

37

observation

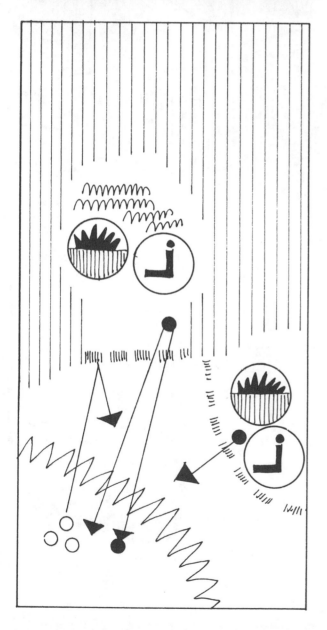

Understanding the thoughts and actions of children can be difficult for adults, particularly those who are not specifically trained in child development. Observation is one means by which they can become familiar with children and their activities. Teachers find observation valuable to them as an aid in improving their methods. Parents also learn how to deal more effectively with their children when they are able to observe them in the learning environment. The values of observation suggest that this activity be accommodated in a special area in the child development center. Probably the main requirements of an observation area are visual access to a variety of children's activities and separation to prevent observers from interfering with the activities they are observing. Opinions vary about the extent of separation between the children and the people observing them. Most authorities agree that separation in terms of distance is necessary. However, some feel that visual separation constitutes an invasion of the children's privacy. Perhaps a combination of both visible and concealed observation areas is an adequate solution.

Design Requirements:

1. Provide for observation of children and teachers in the large group area and a variety of other areas inside and outside of the child development center.
2. Provide both visible and concealed observation areas.
3. Provide comfortable and movable seating for adults in the observation area.
4. Provide writing surfaces in the area.
5. Provide separation between the observation area and other areas in the center in order to prevent mutual interference.

Participants:
staff
parents
consultants

Objectives and Activities:
observation of children's and staff's performance

reading and writing

Language is the externalization of thought. Each word symbolizes a discreet concept. If specific language symbols, words in spoken or written form, are widely understood to be representative of concepts, then these symbols become a medium for thought exchange. During the socialization process, children are introduced to verbal communication when their parents use spoken words to teach them about their environment. Eventually, children acquire the ability to use speech in expressing their own thoughts. A very important task of the child development center is not only to nurture children's speaking skills but also to introduce language in its written form to them. Sophistication in reading and writing is a prerequisite for adequate performance in the social environment. In order to insure children's development of these cognitive skills, an area especially for reading and writing must be included in the center. Development in reading and writing is enhanced when these activities occur in other areas in the center. For example, written labels on items in the environment expand children's vocabularies.

Design Requirements:
1. Provide for quiet individual and group reading in the area.
2. Provide for shared experiences of informal story telling.
3. Provide for written expressions by individuals or small groups.
4. Provide typewriters in the area near a sound absorbing surface.
5. Provide storage in the area that is easily accessible to children and that allows entire book covers to be visible.
6. Provide ample vertical surfaces for display.
7. Provide comfortable, movable seating for children and teachers.
8. Provide a floor surface in the area that encourages lounging.
9. Provide horizontal surfaces for large book reading and display.
10. Provide protection from circulation and other activities.

Objectives:
intellectual stimulation
acquisition of information
emotional development
interplay between reading and experience
skill development

Participants:
children
teacher
teacher assistant

Molecular Activities:
reading, browsing, relaxing, individual, isolation, story telling, typing, looking at displays, noting, relating, writing, dictating

science

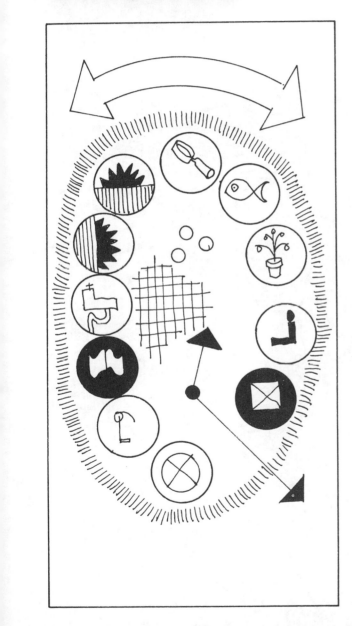

Children come to the child development center equipped with an imaginative curiosity about the world around them. They want to know about heat, water, light, living things, and a wide range of other items and phenomena. A science area integrates natural and man-made objects into the world of children and nurtures their curiosity and understanding of the environment and the interrelationships within it. The information presented to children by displays of plants, animals, and scientific measuring equipment is accentuated by relevant reading material in the science area. Activities in a science area are usually oriented to the individual. For this reason, privacy is an important provision for scientific learning.

Design Requirements:
1. Provide a variety of experiences for investigation of the natural world in the science area.
2. Provide for quiet, individual activity.
3. Provide ample space for display and experimentation that is easily accessible to children.
4. Provide laboratory facilities and equipment in the area.
5. Provide separate containers for different animals.
6. Provide for a minimum of physical contact between children and living things.
7. Provide for all around viewing of natural displays.
8. Provide natural lighting for plants.
9. Provide ample horizontal work surfaces in the science area.
10. Provide comfortable, child sized seating in the area.
11. Provide a sink in the area that is easily accessible to children.
12. Provide lockable storage for some scientific equipment.
13. Provide protection from circulation and other activities.
14. Provide an outdoor space for gardening and animals.

Objectives:
concept formation   problem solving
sensory and perceptual acuity
perpetuate inquiring nature
experimentation

Participants:
children
teacher
teacher assistant

Molecular Activities:
reading
observing
manipulating displays
measuring
maintaining animals and plants
experimenting

manipulative play

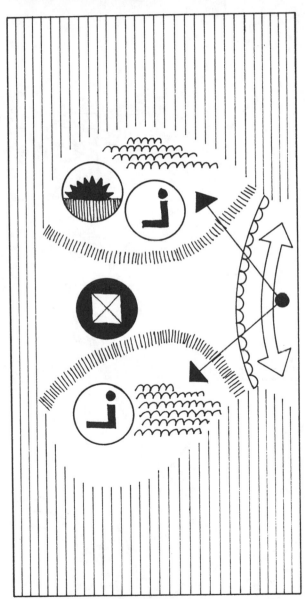

An area especially for manipulative toys is an important provision in a child development center. In this area, children can play with these toys and learn from them without being distracted by other activities in the center. Manipulative toys are intended to present discreet concepts to children. Usually they are designed to eliminate any variables that tend to interfere with their specific purposes. For example, if the concept of shape is intended to be associated with and discovered from a toy, then irrelevant factors such as color and texture are kept constant in the toy so that children cannot confuse shape with other concepts. Such simplification makes learning easy and enjoyable for children. Manipulative toys often require children to operate them manually and with some degree of precision. Puzzles, pegboards, and construction sets are familiar examples of toys that encourage somewhat complex operations. Children learn both about their physical manipulations, and about the relationships resulting from these actions. As a result they develop eye-hand coordination as well as perceptual skills and conceptual knowledge. A manipulative area functions best if it allows privacy for individually oriented activities.

Design Requirements:
1. Provide for quiet, individual play in the manipulative toy area.
2. Provide an open space for small group interaction in the area.
3. Provide a wide variety of manipulative toys.
4. Provide storage that displays these toys and makes them easily accessible to children.
5. Provide movable, comfortable, child sized furniture in the area.
6. Provide flooring in the area that encourages lounging.
7. Provide a high level of lighting in the area.
8. Provide protection from circulation and other activities.

Objectives:
concept formation   positive self-image
sensory and perceptual acuity
eye-hand coordination
visual discrimination   problem solving
small muscle development

Participants:
children
teacher
teacher assistant

Molecular Activities:
handling	listening
arranging	grouping
stacking	
ordering	
combining	
taking apart	

listening

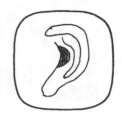

Spoken language is the basis of communication among people. Dependent upon it is practically all childhood socialization and subsequent education. Children cannot begin to learn beyond a physical realm of understanding until their listening and speaking abilities are strong enough to permit them to understand abstract thought. Parents usually train their children to a great extent in understanding and using words as a medium for expression and comprehension. However, the child development center must reinforce for children the listening and speaking abilities they have learned from their parents, polish these abilities, and direct them toward further development. In order to accomplish these goals, it is necessary that a listening area be included in the center. An area specifically for listening helps to broaden children's experiences with sounds and spoken words. Especially important is the provision of tape recorders to allow children to hear their own voices. The area must be somewhat private, but it also must be usable by groups as well as by individuals.

Design Requirements:
1. Provide for quiet individual and group activities in the listening area.
2. Provide listening equipment that is easy for children to operate such as language masters, tape recorders, and a television.
3. Provide cubicles for individual listening in the area.
4. Provide comfortable and movable seating in the area for children and teachers.
5. Provide flooring in the area that encourages lounging.
6. Provide vertical display surfaces in the area.
7. Provide for adult supervision of the listening area.
8. Provide that visual access to the outside does not interfere with listening activities.
9. Provide protection from circulation and other activities.

Objectives:
concept formation
sensory and perceptual acuity
language development
rhythm development

Participants:
children
teacher
teacher assistant

Molecular Activities:
listening   watching television
speaking   operating equipment
taking out/putting away equipment

mathematics

Mathematics involves thought in perhaps its most abstract form. Since children must learn to think abstractly as well as intuitively and concretely, it is logical for mathematics to be included as a learning experience in the child development center. An area for this activity provides children with materials and supplementary reading which enables them to relate their personal learning experiences to the logic of mathematical knowledge. A mathematics area functions best if it provides privacy for individually oriented activities.

Design Requirements:
1. Provide a variety of materials to encourage mathematical exploration.
2. Provide for quiet, individual activities which involve classification, seriation, and one to one correspondence.
3. Provide for close adult assistance and intervention when necessary.
4. Provide ample display space in the mathematics area.
5. Provide writing surfaces and comfortable seating for children in the area.
6. Provide a floor covering in the area that encourages lounging.
7. Provide protection from circulation and other activities.

Objectives:
concept formation   problem solving
sensory and perceptual acuity

Participants:
children
teacher
teacher assistant

Molecular Activities:
reading
observing
ordering
relating
measuring
classifying
counting
manipulating

concept formation

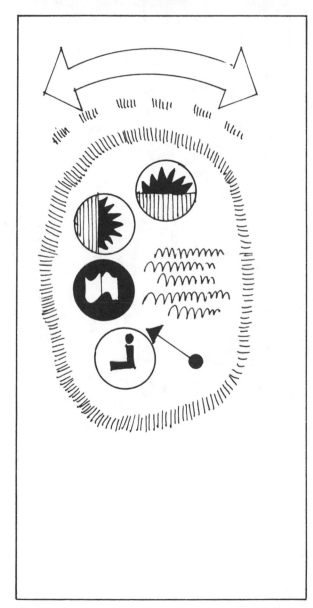

Although concept formation is a consequence of many different activities in the child development center, a special area devoted to the presentation of specific concepts is an important part of the center. In the concept formation area, exhibits and relevant books emphasize a single concept isolated so that children can understand its meaning clearly. Geometric shape, color, and distance are a few of many concepts that can be presented. Children can relate these specific concepts to their discoveries in other activities. Exhibits in the area are changed periodically so that children can be exposed in depth to a variety of different concepts. Concept formation is a somewhat individual activity. However, the area must accommodate varying numbers of children and can well be a focal point of the child development center.

Design Requirements:
1. Provide for the formation of a variety of specific concepts by periodically changing the displays in the concept formation area.
2. Provide books in the area to emphasize the particular concept being presented.
3. Provide for quiet, individual activities in the concept formation area.
4. Provide enough space in the area so that many children can participate simultaneously.
5. Provide ample horizontal and vertical display surfaces in the area.
6. Provide protection from circulation and other activities.

Objectives:
concept formation   language development
sensory and perceptual acuity

Participants:
children
teacher
teacher assistant

Molecular Activities:
sitting
handling
displaying
taking apart
feeling
tasting
looking
listening

FRANCE

large group

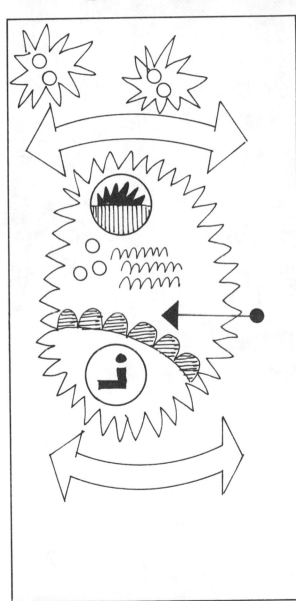

An area where all the children can come together at one time for large group activities such as dancing, watching films, or talking with their teachers as a group is essential to the child development center. When all the children can be together, they develop a strong sense of group solidarity. Flexibility is an important characteristic in this area. It must be adaptable to a wide variety of activities and also must **accommodate** activities that occasionally expand into it from the smaller learning centers. Openness and a very social atmosphere are desirable qualities in a large group area.

Design Requirements:
1. Provide easy access to the large group area from the smaller learning centers.
2. Provide a focal point in the area in order to control the children's attention.
3. Provide flooring in the area that encourages lounging and reduces noise.
4. **Provide for darkening the large group area for slide shows or films.**
5. Provide for adult supervision of the area.
6. Provide for circulation flow around the edges of the large group area in order to prevent activity fragmentation.
7. Provide visual access to the outside from the area.

Objectives:
individual functioning as a group member
group solidarity
language development

Participants:
children
teacher
teacher assistant
visitors
parents

Molecular Activities:
playing alone
playing in groups
reading
listening
dramatization
special group activities

SCHOOL OF EDUCATION
CURRICULUM LABORATORY
UM-DEARBORN

art

The art work of children is a visual expression of their feelings about experiences which are personally significant to them. These feelings they choose to express can result from direct involvement in home or school activities or from vicarious experiences in listening to stories and reading. In order to express their thoughts visually, children must think about themselves and their physical and social environment. For this reason, art activities are valuable for intellectual development and for self image formation. Art can mean invention to children, and thus it becomes important for self expression, communication, and problem solving. Working individually and controlling their own actions, children learn technical skills and gain self reliance and positive self-images. Variety in art activities is limited only by the teacher's choice of materials to make available for the children's use. Among many common art media are painting with brushes and fingers, paper cutting and pasting, and clay modelling. An art area must be usable both by individuals and by groups without significant interference.

Design Requirements:
1. Provide for both individual and group activities in the art area.
2. Provide both vertical and horizontal work surfaces with ample space around them for activity.
3. Provide storage for these materials that is easily accessible to children.
4. Provide storage that is inaccessible to children.
5. Provide storage for incomplete art projects.
6. Provide a space for drying art work.
7. Provide for separation of incompatible art activities.
8. Provide a washing facility in the area, preferably a sink with a drainboard, that is easily accessible to children.
9. Provide flooring in the area that is easily cleanable and impervious to art materials such as paint and clay.
10. Provide visual access to the outside.
11. Provide protection from circulation and other activities.

Objectives:
positive self-image
sensory and perceptual acuity
eye-hand coordination
small muscle development
self expression
visual discrimination

Participants:
children, teacher, teacher assistant

Molecular Activities:
finger painting, brush/easel painting, collage, paper mache, cutting, pasting, drawing/coloring, clay modelling, mural making, cleaning up, washing, mixing

cooking

Cooking can be a valuable experience for children. Not only does this useful production give children satisfaction and a sense of responsibility, but also the activity is important for learning. For example, concepts about shapes and other properties of food can be formed as a result of involvement in cooking activities. Scraping and slicing vegetables require children to manipulate them with some degree of skill thus developing eye-hand coordination. Cooking also is a natural socializing activity that encourages the individual to participate in groups. An area for this activity must have enough space to accommodate several children simultaneously.

Design Requirements:
1. Provide both hot and cold food preparation equipment that is easy for children to handle in the cooking area.
2. Provide facilities for dish washing in the area.
3. Provide facilities for waste disposal.
4. Provide waterproof and easily cleanable working surfaces in the area.
5. Provide for storage and display of cooking utensils.
6. Provide protection from circulation and other activities.
7. Provide ventilation for the cooking area.
8. Provide visual access to the outside in the area.

Objectives:
eye-hand coordination   problem solving
concept formation
small muscle development
socializing   language development

Participants:
children
teacher
teacher assistant

Molecular Activities:
pouring
stirring
tasting
mixing
cooking
eating
measuring

eating

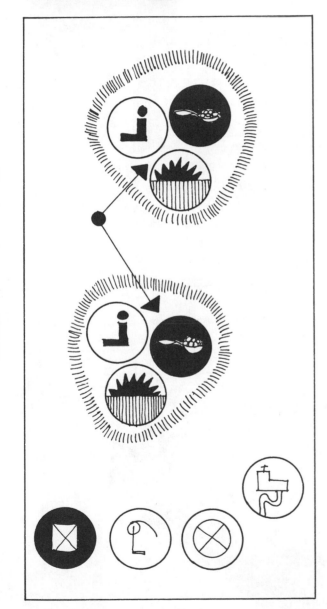

Occasionally children come to the child development center without having eaten earlier at home. Also, they usually develop healthy appetites as a result of active play. For these reasons, it is necessary that a time for eating be included in the center's schedule each day. Food gives children extra energy and frees them to become fully involved in learning activities. Moreover, eating itself can be a significant learning experience. It offers many opportunities for children to explore concepts such as color and texture in the foods they eat. Equally important is the chance it provides for children to learn about unfamiliar foods. Socialization in acceptable eating habits comes as a result of observing teachers and other children while they eat. Children also learn to take responsibility when they serve food and clean up. Children enjoy eating in small groups throughout the center, so that a specific eating place perhaps is unnecessary.

Design Requirements:
1. Provide a variety of settings in the child development center where small groups of children and adults can eat.
2. Provide an area where food can be distributed.
3. Provide comfortable, child sized tables and seating that can be cleaned easily.
4. Provide for family style serving in large bowls.
5. Provide utensils that can be used easily by children.
6. Provide storage that is easily accessible to children for food they bring from home.
7. Provide easily accessible facilities for hand washing.
8. Provide waste receptacles for excess food and disposable utensils.

Objectives:
concept formation
sensory and perceptual acuity
eye-hand coordination
socialization   language development

Participants:
children
teacher
teacher assistants
visitors

Molecular Activities:
serving food
drinking
eating
cleaning up

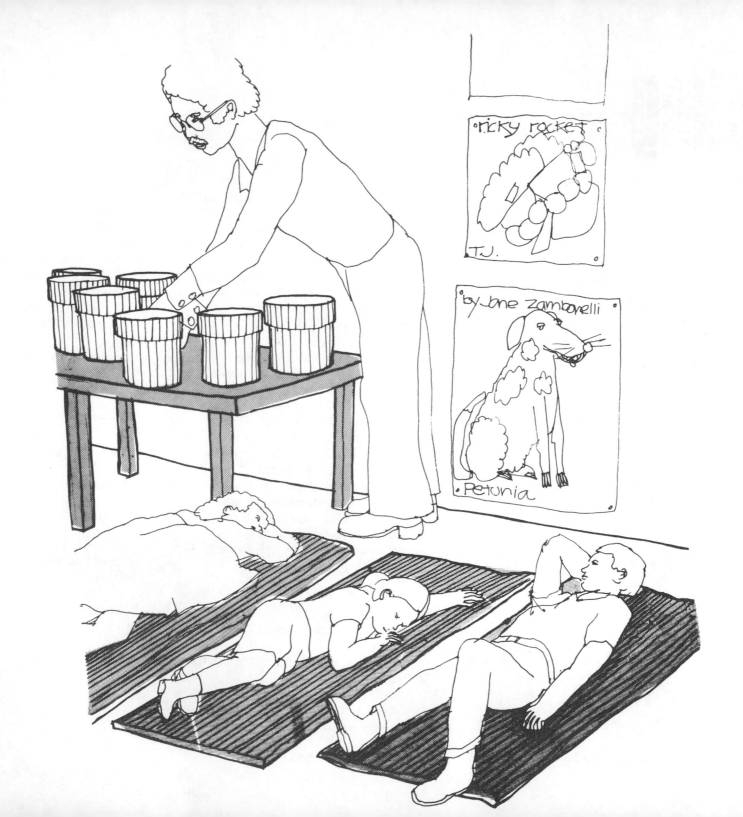

ricky rocket

TJ.

by Jane Zamborelli

Petunia

58

napping

Provisions for sleeping vary among child development centers due mainly to the length of time the children stay at the centers. Relatively long sleeping periods or short napping periods may be included, or it may be that no specific periods for rest are scheduled at all. However, provisions are necessary if only to give children an opportunity to rest from active play and to freshen themselves for more activity later in the day. Due to the variations in children's resting habits, it is necessary that the activity be an opportunity and not a requirement. Sleeping usually does not require a special space, but it is very individually oriented and private.

Design Requirements:
1. Provide for quiet, individual passivity in sleeping.
2. Provide pads or cots for sleeping.
3. Provide storage for sleeping equipment that is easily accessible to children.
4. Provide for warm flooring if pads are used.
5. Provide for darkening in sleeping areas.
6. Provide space for adult supervision of sleeping and circulation among children.
7. Provide protection from the noise of circulation and other activities.

Participants:
children
teacher
teacher assistant

Molecular Activities:
sleeping
resting
quiet play
whispering
reading
setting up cots or pads
getting cots or pads
storing linens

water play

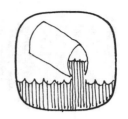

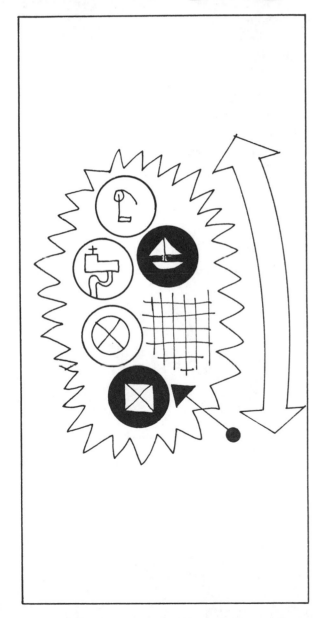

Flexibility in form and function is a primary characteristic of water, and because of its flexibility, it offers children many opportunities for experimentation. Water play, therefore, is important for concept formation. While children splash, they can observe the phenomenon of waves. Playing with toys in the water and measuring introduce to children concepts of floating, sinking, and quantity. These activities are only a few examples of the discovery and learning that occur during water play. Just as important is the pleasure children have in stimulating their senses and feeling. Water play tends to be a group activity. For this reason, an area for this activity requires enough space to accommodate varying numbers of children.

Design Requirements:
1. Provide a water receptacle as deep and as large in water surface area as possible.
2. Provide enough area around the receptacle so that numbers of children can participate in water play simultaneously.
3. Provide an ample supply of props for water play.
4. Provide storage for props that is easily accessible to children.
5. Provide for a minimum of water spillage.
6. Provide waterproof and slip-proof surfaces in the area.
7. Provide some means for keeping children's clothing dry such as waterproof aprons.
8. Provide towels that are easily accessible to children.
9. Provide facilities for hose connection.
10. Provide an exterior view in the area.
11. Provide as much natural lighting as possible in the water play area.
12. Provide for adult supervision in the area.
13. Provide adequate heating in the area.
14. Provide protection from circulation and other activities.

Objectives:
concept formation
sensory and perceptual acuity
eye-hand coordination
small muscle development

Participants:
children
teacher
teacher assistant

Molecular Activities:
pouring
floating/sinking
blowing bubbles
splashing
washing
measuring
beating
coloring
standing/sitting in water

toilet

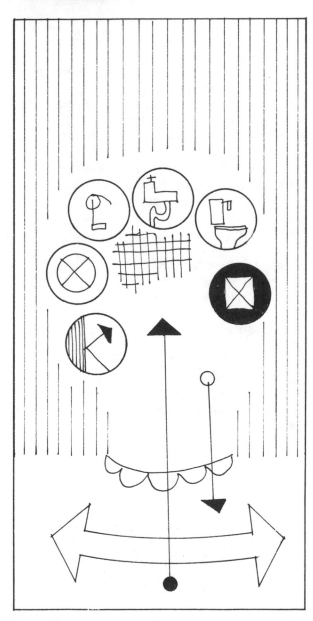

It is obvious that easily accessible toilet facilities for children are a necessity in a child development center. However, pleasure as well as necessity is an important consideration in a toilet area. A sociable, enjoyable atmosphere is desirable to make toileting a pleasure. This quality can be facilitated by the use of bright colors, sunlight, and views to outdoor areas. Although most educators suggest that privacy and separation of the sexes be minimized in toilet areas, provisions for privacy vary from center to center.

Design Requirements:
1. Provide toilets, urinals, and lavatories that are the correct size and height for children.
2. Provide easily accessible toilet paper and towels for hand drying.
3. Provide mirrors in the area at child height.
4. Provide seamless surfaces that are waterproof and easily cleanable in the area.
5. Provide for easy accessibility to the toilet area from all play areas both inside and outside of the center.
6. Provide for adult accessibility to the area.
7. Provide sound isolation so that activities in the area do not interfere with other activities.
8. Provide as much natural lighting in the toilet area as possible.
9. Provide visual access to the outside.

Participants:
children
teacher
teacher assistant

Molecular Activities:
toileting
dressing/undressing
washing/drying hands
looking in mirrors

classroom wash

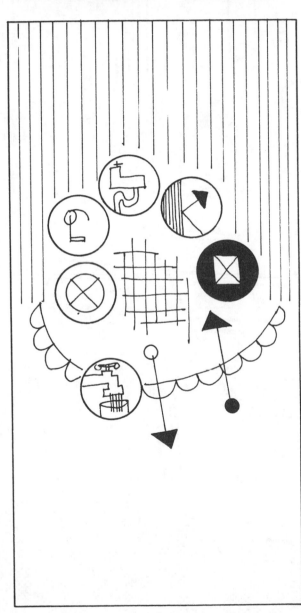

Several washing functions are served by a classroom wash area. Perhaps most important is hand cleaning associated with active play. Children get dirty during play and also have accidents such as spills that require washing. Also, children usually wash after toileting and before eating. It is not necessary for this activity to be limited to one particular area. Washing can be decentralized in order to be more closely related to active play areas in the child development center.

Design Requirements:
1. Provide sinks both for adults and for children in the wash area.
2. Provide towels at a location that is easily accessible to children.
3. Provide a child sized drinking fountain in the area.
4. Provide mirrors above the sinks so that children can see themsleves.
5. Provide water temperature controls in order to avoid scalding.
6. Provide storage and facilities for cleaning muddy boots, umbrellas, etc.
7. Provide surfaces in the area that are waterproof and easily cleanable.
8. Provide for adult supervision of the area.
9. Provide for draft minimization in the wash area.
10. Provide easy accessibility to the wash area from other activity areas both inside the center and outdoors.

Participants:
children
teacher
teacher assistant

Molecular Activities:
drinking
washing hands
cleaning objects
looking in mirrors

SCHOOL OF EDUCATION
CURRICULUM LABORATORY
UM-DEARBORN

indoor active play

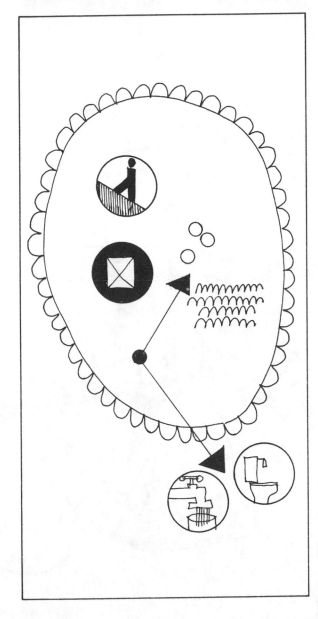

Children tend to become excessively active and excited. Under usual circumstances they are able to exercise and reduce their excitement during active outdoor play. However, problems arise when weather conditions such as cold and dampness prevent normal outdoor activities. Children still must have some means of releasing energy. The solution to problems of limited outdoor play is a provision for active play inside the child development center. An indoor area can provide children with a variety of activities for energy release and large muscle development. Climbing and active games are two types of play that can be facilitated in the area. An important environmental requirement of the area is that it be acoustically isolated from the rest of the center. The area must also accommodate a large number of children simultaneously.

Design Requirements:
1. Provide for a variety of activities in the indoor active play area.
2. Provide an open space in the area for active games.
3. Provide a facility for climbing in the area.
4. Provide equipment for active games.
5. Provide easily accessible storage in the area for equipment.
6. Provide flooring in the indoor active play area that reduces noise and prevents falling accidents.
7. Provide acoustic separation between the active play area and other areas in the child development center.
8. Provide for adult supervision of the area.

Objectives:
large muscle development
eye-hand coordination
positive self-image
problem solving
concept formation
sensory development

Participants:
children
teacher
teacher assistant

Molecular Activities:
bending
squatting
crawling
climbing
stretching
balancing
falling
jumping
cooperating
running

block play

Block play serves various functions in the development of children. Building structures from blocks is one way in which children express themselves. Their expressions may be either abstract or representational. When children explore their personal ideas structurally, they observe physical principles and form concepts of size, weight, shape, and fit. Moreover, they must use their newly formed concepts in making decisions about what to build and how to proceed in building it. Interest, then, is in the process of building rather than in the final product. Children gain confidence and sense of achievement when they become skilled enough to build large, complex structures. Block play typically assumes two somewhat incompatible forms, active and passive in character. Often associated with the use of large blocks, active block play involves an aggressive use of power by children in testing themselves against their environment. However, children also like to retreat from their environment, and the use of small blocks is individually oriented to an extent that it is suitable activity for children seeking refuge.

Design Requirements:

1. Provide blocks that encourage balancing and climbing.
2. Provide ample and flexible space for large scale, active block play.
3. Provide protected spaces for passive, individual block play.
4. Provide storage for blocks that presents their building potential and that is easily accessible to children.
5. Provide display space for completed structures in the area.
6. Provide vertical display surfaces in the area.
7. Provide flooring and work surfaces in the area that reduce impact noise.
8. Provide separation between block play and other quieter activities.
9. Provide protection from circulation.

Objectives:

concept formation   problem solving
large/small muscle development
self expression   positive self-image
eye-hand coordination
visual discrimination

Participants:

children
teacher
teacher assistant

Molecular Activities:

building, stocking, arranging, destroying structures, balancing, climbing, taking out/ putting away equipment

construction

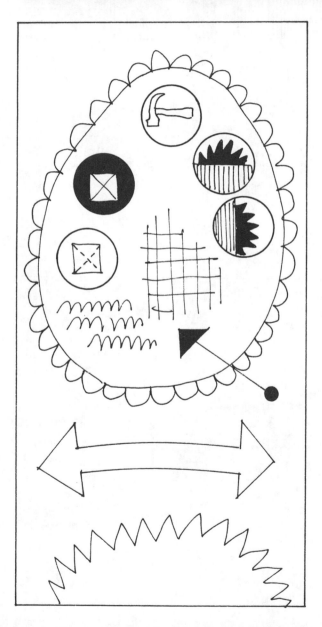

Children delight in building activities in a construction area. Hammering, sawing, and drilling allow them to release energy and hostility constructively. Moreover, such physical activity develops large and small muscles, eye-hand coordination, and visual acuity. Just as important to children is a development of confidence in their improving tool handling skills and pride in the objects they create. Construction activities are very active and noisy, and for this reason it is necessary that a construction area be separated acoustically from other activities in the child development center. Space in the area must be adequate for the simultaneous use of numbers of children.

Design Requirements:

1. Provide a variety of tools that are safe for children to use in the construction area.
2. Provide wood, nails, and other materials for building.
3. Provide horizontal work surfaces in the area with ample space for activity around them.
4. Provide storage that displays tools and building materials and that is easily accessible to children.
5. Provide ample space for displaying completed projects.
6. Provide flooring and work surfaces that reduce impact noise and that are easily cleanable of splinters and nails.
7. Provide for constant adult supervision of the area.
8. Provide easy access to first aid in the area.
9. Provide an acoustical separation between noisy construction activities and other quieter activities in the center.
10. Provide protection from circulation and other activities.

Objectives:
concept formation
large/small muscle development
self-expression
eye-hand coordination
visual discrimination
positive self-image
problem solving

Participants:
children
teacher
teacher assistant

Molecular Activities:
hammering
sawing
drilling
taking out/putting away equipment

dramatic play

Fascinated by the experiences of everyday life, children enjoy interpreting these experiences and re-enacting them. For example, children assume adult roles in dramatic play and recreate a wide variety of behavioral situations involving role relationships. Among many common dramatic activities are housekeeping, shop keeping, and transportation play. The importance of dramatic play lies in children's development in understanding themselves and others and in their gaining confidence that they can be whatever they wish to be. Experiences are widened when children are allowed to act out new roles and situations they encounter. Also, dramatic play encourages development toward sophistication in oral expression. This activity usually is group oriented. However, it is necessary that a space for dramatic play provide some degree of privacy.

Design Requirements:
1. Provide for a wide range of dramatic activities by keeping a large variety of props and toys available to children.
2. Provide materials to allow children to create their own props for special activities.
3. Provide an area that can function as a stage for dramatic presentations.
4. Provide a full length mirror so that children can see themselves in role oriented costumes.
5. Provide storage for dramatic equipment that is easily accessible to children.
6. Provide a ceiling system that permits the hanging of lightweight props.
7. Provide lighting that can be directed toward the area specifically for dramatic presentations.
8. Provide flooring that reduces noise in the dramatic area.
9. Provide protection from circulation and other activities.

Objectives:
positive self-image   social development
language development
role enactments
orientation in fantasy and reality

Participants:
children
teacher
teacher assistant

Molecular Activities:
dress up
puppetry
household
fire station
grocery store
hospital
special activities
setting up props
making special props
dramatic presentation

music

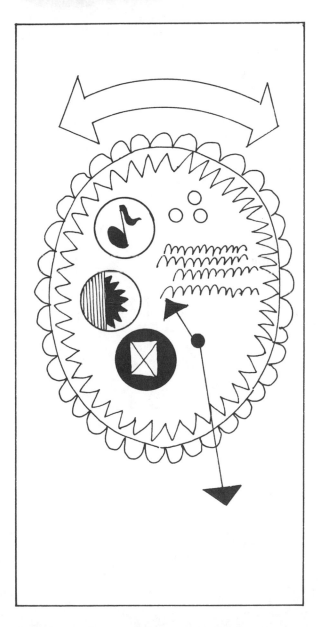

Musical interest is quite evident in the activities of children. It is desirable for a child development center to nurture this interest by emphasizing music as a daily activity. Making music and responding to it enhance intellectual, emotional, and social development in children. For example, singing is an important aid to the growth of language abilities. Also, it can be used to introduce and reinforce concepts. Singing, playing instruments, and dancing--natural group activities--teach children to cooperate with others in their social environment. Equally important is the pleasure children experience in making sounds and expressing their own musical ideas. Since musical play usually involves groups, it is essential that a music area accommodate varying numbers of children.

Design Requirements:
1. Provide for group activities in the music area.
2. Provide ample space for body movement.
3. Provide for informal singing in the area.
4. Provide for experimentation with instrumental noises.
5. Provide musical equipment that is easy for children to operate.
6. Provide for display of various musical instruments.
7. Provide storage for records and instruments that is easily accessible to children.
8. Provide flooring in the area that encourages lounging and reduces noise.
9. Provide for adult supervision of the music area.
10. Provide separation between the music area and other areas to prevent mutual interference.

Objectives:
concept formation
sensory and perceptual acuity
language development
rhythm and balance development
emotional development
social development

Participants:
children
teacher
teacher assistant

Molecular Activities:
listening
relaxing
composing
singing
dancing
operating equipment
handling instruments
manipulation

visual aids

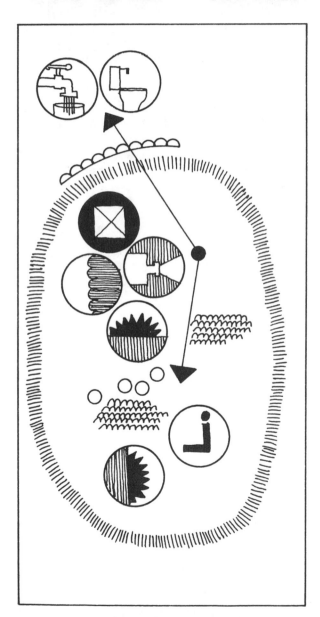

Viewing slides and films can add depth and scope to children's learning experiences. For example, this activity can be an important supplement to field trips or group listening and story telling. It can also introduce to children experiences that may not be accessible through reading or instruction. Consequently, it can give children valuable information and stimulate their intellectual development. The advantages of learning from visual aids warrant the inclusion of this activity in the child development center. Film viewing is usually a group activity, and therefore it requires a space large enough for a number of children. However, this activity does not require a special area in the center. Perhaps the large group area is best suited for learning from visual aids.

Design Requirements:
1. Provide space for a large group of participants.
2. Provide for darkening in the area.
3. Provide for quietness in the area.
4. Provide a large, light colored, vertical surface for showing slides and films.
5. Provide equipment for projecting slides and films.
6. Provide lockable storage for projection equipment.
7. Provide flooring in the area that encourages lounging.

Objectives:
intellectual development
language development
concept formation

Participants:
children
teacher
teacher assistant

Molecular Activities:
listening
questioning
viewing slides and films

locker wrapping

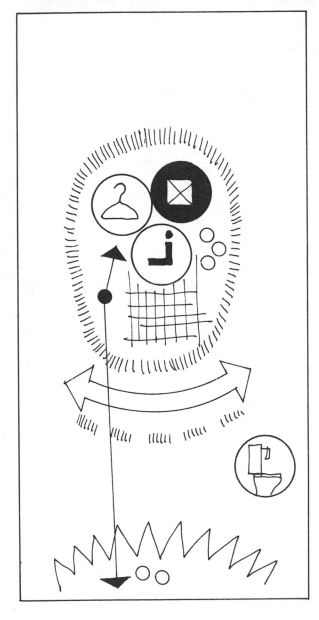

A locker-wrapping area functions specifically for the storage of extra clothing such as coats and boots that children do not wear inside the child development center. However, it is necessary that this clothing remain available to children during the day for outdoor play. Numbers of children dress and undress in the area simultaneously, so that it must be large enough to accommodate them.

Design Requirements:
1. Provide storage for wraps, boots, etc. that is easily accessible to children.
2. Provide for ventilation of wet clothing.
3. Provide storage for clean clothing.
4. Provide some child sized seating in the locker-wrapping area.
5. Provide waterproof, slip-proof, and easily cleanable flooring in the area.
6. Provide for adult supervision of the area.
7. Provide easy access to toilets and to the outdoor play area.
8. Provide separation between activities in the locker-wrapping area and other activities to prevent interference.

Participants:
children
teacher
teacher assistant
mothers

Molecular Activities:
taking off/putting on wraps
carrying personal items
storing personal items
handling parcels
talking
waiting
helping

cubby

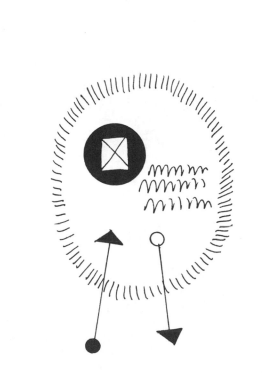

When a child has a private space to store personal items — a cubby — and when he sees his name labelling that space, he gains a feeling of self importance. It is therefore apparent that storage of this nature serves a mental function as well as the utilitarian function of housing a child's private possessions. A cubby area differs from a locker wrapping area in that storage here is for smaller items not necessarily associated with outdoor activities. For example, items may be art work or lunches brought from home. **The cubby area must accommodate many** children; however, activity in the area is individually oriented and private.

Design Requirements:
1. Provide independent storage spaces for each child's personal possessions that are easily accessible to children.
2. Provide for name labelling of each storage space.
3. Provide easy access to the cubby area from other activity areas in the center.

Objectives:
positive self-image
personal storage

Participants:
children

Molecular Activities:
dressing/undressing
taking out/putting away items
storing personal possessions

OUTDOOR PLAY

protected outdoor play

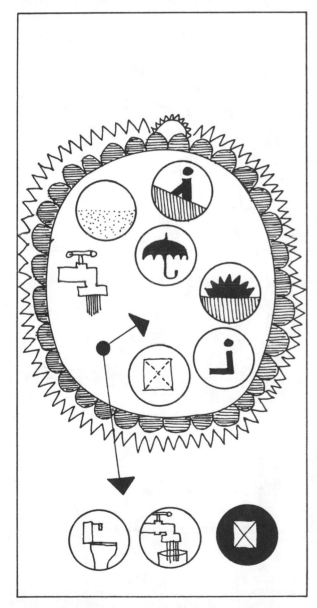

A very desirable part of the outdoor play environment is an area covered by permanent roofing. Such an area allows children to play actively outdoors when weather conditions prevent them from playing in unprotected areas. Another function of this area is of acting as an extension to the indoor play environment. Excessively noisy activities, for instance, can be moved to the covered outdoor area when they are disturbing quieter activities inside. A covered outdoor space must have enough area to accommodate large groups of children.

Design Requirements:
1. Provide for a wide variety of activities in the protected outdoor play area.
2. Provide a permanent roof to protect the area.
3. Provide screening for protection on the sides of the area.
4. Provide for a minimum of structural supports in the area's interior.
5. Provide lockable storage space for movable playground equipment away from the protected outdoor play area.
6. Provide for adult supervision of the area.
7. Provide easy access to toilets and drinking fountains.

Objectives:
concept formation
sensory and perceptual acuity
large/small muscle development
positive self-image

Participants:
children
teacher
teacher assistant

Molecular Activities:
construction
running
jumping
crawling
rolling
climbing
riding
rope jumping
balancing
pushing/pulling
throwing
cooperating

upen outduur play

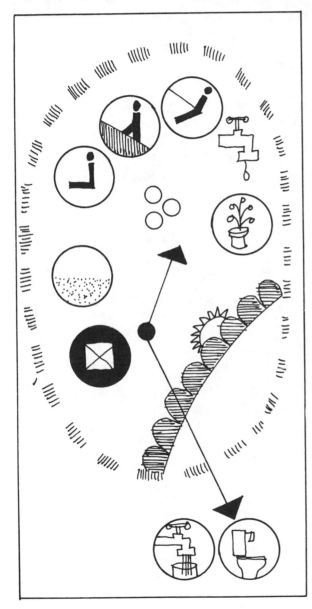

Vigorous exercise and social interaction characterize children's activities in an outdoor open space. This outdoor play is essential for the development of large and small muscles and the coordination of eyes and body parts. Primarily a group activity, outdoor play is important for social development. Children learn to cooperate with one another when they play together as a group. Outdoor play also offers valuable opportunities for nature study. Many different activities occur during outdoor play. For example, children run, jump rope, climb, and swing. Children choose the level of difficulty they want and gradually progress to more complex activities. In this way, they gradually increase their coordination and muscular skills. In order for outdoor areas to become effective extensions of the indoor learning environment, it is necessary that children have free access to these areas at any time during the day.

Design Requirements:
1. Provide a wide variety of playground equipment that requires different levels of movement skills and that is safe for children to use.
2. Provide sequences of different activities that require quick changes in muscle use.
3. Provide spatial variety in the open outdoor play area.
4. Provide several different kinds of playing surfaces such as grass, soil and concrete in the area.
5. Provide soft ground cover around the playground equipment to prevent falling accidents.
6. Provide child sized seating in the open area.
7. Provide adequate and lockable storage space for movable playground equipment.
8. Provide a means of enclosure for the area so that children will not wander away.
9. Provide for adult supervision of the area.
10. Provide easy access to toilets and drinking fountains.

Objectives:
concept formation
sensory and perceptual acuity
large/small muscle development
positive self-image

Participants:
children
teacher
teacher assistant

Molecular Activities:
running, jumping, crawling, rolling, climbing, riding, rope jumping, balancing, pushing/pulling, cooperating, throwing.

sand

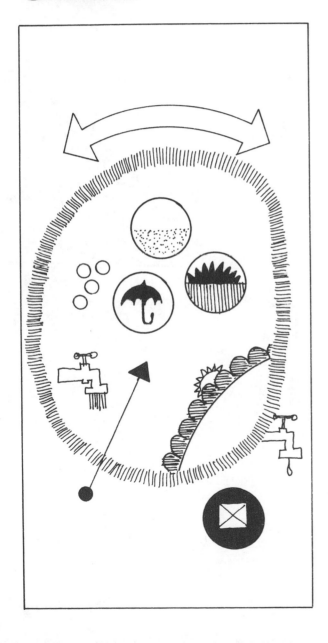

Sand is a very flexible material for manipulative play--children can sift, mold, pour, and measure it. These activities help children to learn about sand itself and allow them to discover concepts of quantity and spatial relationship. Especially enjoyable to children as a means for self expression, sand play satisfies their needs to invent, to explore new ideas, and to solve problems. Physical exercise of large and small muscles and experiences in group cooperativeness are other values that children gain from this activity. In order to encourage grouping, an area for sand play must accommodate several children simultaneously. However, provisions for the needs of children who wish to play individually must also be made. Although sand play is traditionally associated with the outdoors, this activity can easily occur inside a child development center. In this case easy maintenance is an important consideration for the design of a sand area.

Design Requirements:
1. Provide for both indoor and outdoor sand play.
2. Provide for group activities in the sand area.
3. Provide non-overlapping areas with ample space for individual activities.
4. Provide a physical boundary around the sand area to keep the sand in place.
5. Provide a water source that is easily accessible to children in the area.
6. Provide sufficient drainage for the sand area.
7. Provide horizontal working surfaces near the sand.
8. Provide storage for toys that is easily accessible to children in the area.
9. Provide scuffing surfaces for shoe cleaning near the sand area.
10. Provide protection from rain in outdoor sand areas.
11. Provide partial shading for outdoor sand areas.

Objectives:
concept formation
sensory and perceptual acuity
large/small muscle development
positive self-image

Participants:
children
teacher
teacher assistant

Molecular Activities:
bending   sitting
squatting   touching
crawling   measuring
digging   wetting
forming
lifting
carrying

swinging

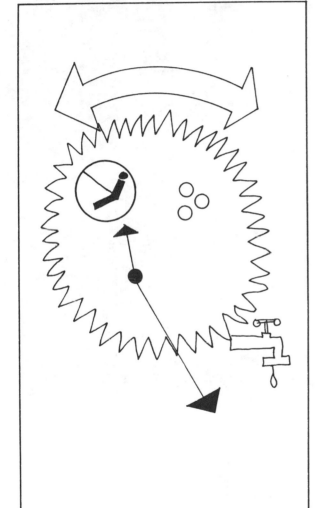

Children enjoy swinging as a part of outdoor play. Not only is this activity enjoyable, but also it is important to children as a means of developing large and small muscles. Children also gain personal courage from swinging when they meet the challenge of swinging increasingly higher. This activity usually is experienced individually. However, small group interaction occurs when children cooperate with each other in the use of swinging facilities.

Design Requirements:
1. Provide swinging equipment that is safe and enjoyable for children to use.
2. Provide a soft and well drained area around the swings to prevent falling accidents.
3. Provide for adult supervision of the swing area.
4. Provide protection from objects, circulation, and other activities.

Objectives:
concept formation
large/small muscle development
emotional development

Participants:
children

Molecular Activities:
jumping
pushing
pulling
balancing
hanging
sliding
falling
cooperating

SCHOOL OF EDUCATION
CURRICULUM LABORATORY
UM-DEARBORN

climbing

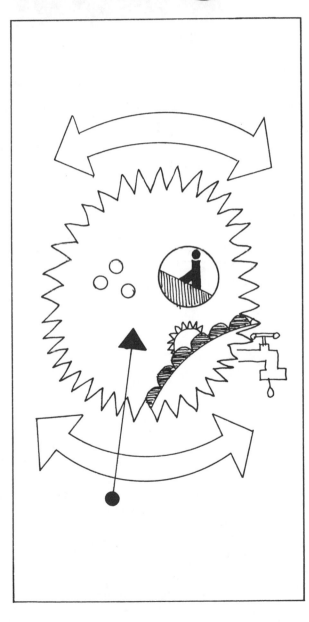

Climbing is an important part of outdoor play. The values it offers children lie primarily in large muscle development and eye-hand coordination. Moreover, children find it especially enjoyable. The activity becomes a challenge for them when the climbing apparatus provides progressively difficult situations to master. Climbing can also be an enjoyable activity inside the child development center. It can easily be included in the indoor active play area. Climbing is individually oriented, but equipment for it must accommodate numbers of children simultaneously.

Design Requirements:
1. Provide for climbing activities both indoors and outdoors.
2. Provide climbing equipment that is both safe and enjoyable for children to use.
3. Provide for progressively difficult climbing situations.
4. Provide a soft surface around the climbing equipment to prevent falling accidents.
5. Provide for adult supervision of the climbing area.
6. Provide protection from circulation and other activities.

Objectives:
concept formation
eye-hand coordination
large muscle development
emotional development

Participants:
children

Molecular Activities:
reaching
stretching
climbing
hanging
balancing
falling

evaluation chart

ACTIVITY FACTORS	SAND	CLIMBING	SWINGING	OPEN
Run	—	—	—	X
Jump	—	X	—	X
Bend	X	X	—	X
Squat	X	X	—	X
Stretch	X	X	X	X
Pull	X	X	X	X
Push	X	—	X	X
Crawl	X	X	—	X
Swing	—	X	X	—
Climb	X	X	X	X
Balance	X	X	X	X
Dig	X	—	—	—
Carry	X	—	—	X
Lift	X	—	—	X
Throw	—	—	—	X
Roll	X	—	—	X
Sit	X	X	X	X
Imagination	X	X	—	X
Cooperation	X	X	X	X
Planning	X	X	—	X
Social Play	X	X	X	X
Solitary Play	X	X	X	X
Sight	X	X	—	X
Sound [1]	—	—	—	—
Touch	X	X	X	X
Small Muscle Activity	X	X	—	X
Personal Courage	—	X	X	X
Fact Learning	X	X	X	X
Hand-Eye Coordination	X	X	X	X
Spatial Relations	X	X	—	X

[1]Sound experiences can be built into any area as an added detail.

This chart contains a list of activity factors to be covered by a basic outdoor play area. The designations indicate how sand, climbing, swinging and open areas equipped as described meet these requirements (adopted from *A Small World of Play and Learning,* the LINC Childrens Center, North Carolina).

playground planning

Planning Outdoor Play (POP) is a method of facilitating the design of children's outdoor play and the selection of appropriate equipment.

POP consists of four (4) sets of card categories:

OBJECTIVES: The purpose of outdoor play.
ACTIVITIES: What children do outdoors.
ZONES: Areas of related outdoor activities.
SETTINGS: Equipment used by children.

You will need to supply your own cards in a similar manner to the **Planning Environments for Children** game.

The game is to be played by a group of three to five people, although many groups may participate at the same time. To begin, each person selects, from the list provided, no more than four *OBJECTIVES* which seem to be most important. Brief notes should be made justifying each choice. After each person has made his/her choices, individual lists are pooled, and the corresponding *OBJECTIVE* cards are pulled from the deck. *OBJECTIVE* cards are arranged, face up, so they can be seen by all. Through collaboration, the group must choose from these no more than four *OBJECTIVE* cards. Players are urged to forcefully support their individual choices. Continue discussions until consensus is reached on the four *OBJECTIVES* your group feels are most important. After completing this phase, group members should record the final choices on the record sheet.

Next, as a group, examine each *OBJECTIVE* individually, and select three *ACTIVITIES* that can be used to accomplish each

OBJECTIVE. (You should work through each *OBJECTIVE* completely before starting a new one.) Keep in mind that some *ACTIVITIES* may be used with more than one *OBJECTIVE.*

Now, as a group, rearrange all of the *ACTIVITY* cards that have been selected so they appear to fit into an appropriate *ZONE.* It is important to note that not all of the *ZONE* cards need to be used. Record all selection.

Finally, select the appropriate *SETTING* that corresponds with each of the *ACTIVITY* choices and record the number of the *SETTING.*

This set of rules is only a guide for gaining insight into the planning process. Players should feel free to change the rules in order to accommodate more specific needs.

OBJECTIVES	ACTIVITIES
	mixing
	feeling
concept formation	hitting
	crawling
cooperation	splashing
problem solving	role playing
emotional development	dressing up
	molding
self confidence	animals
language development	digging
sensory discrimination	climbing
	painting
self motivation	cooking
social development	pouring
	stretching
initiative	sliding
communication	constructing
self expression	planting
	swinging
positive self-image	throwing
perceptual development	balancing
sensory development	bicycling

private play zone - children use small protected areas for individual or quiet activities.

dramatic play zone - children exercise their imaginations to create roles.

adventure play zone - children spontaneously build and rebuild their environment.

manipulative coordination zone - children develop coordination skills frequently with repetitive motion.

open area play zone - children use large spaces for group games and individual activities, which may require hard or soft surfaces.

creative play zone - children combine materials to make a different object.

large muscle development zone - children overcome physical and mental obstacles, exercising all possible muscles.

nature zone - children interact with natural objects.

imaginative play zone - children exercise imagination and limited muscular effort, but no object is necessarily produced.

Zones	Activities	Equip- ment
Creative Play Zone		
Imaginative Play Zone		
Dramatic Play Zone		
Nature Zone		
Adventure Play Zone		
Private Play Zone		
Manipulative Coordination Zone		
Large Muscle Development Zone		
Open Area Play Zone		

Record Sheet

Objectives

a _____

b _____

c _____

d _____

Activities

a	b
1	1
2	2
3	3

c	d
1	1
2	2
3	3

Equipment

spatial layout

This procedure can be a useful approach for organizing playground layout ideas. It can aid you in discovering various problems that may arise before you actually build and locate the equipment.

You will, however, require the results from Planning Outdoor Play to initiate this procedure. All of the concepts generated by the POP game, particularly the use of Equipment Settings and Zones, will be applied in this exercise. There are two stages to this process: Preparation and Planning.

Preparation

Find a sheet of paper at least 12 inches by 17 inches to draw a ½ inch square grid; or a sheet of graph paper with a ½ inch grid already printed. You will also require the use of the Equipment Settings which should be xeroxed and cut along the solid lines. The drawings were made to scale to fit the ½ inch grid which corresponds to four feet.

Measure the length and width of your playground and record this information on the grided sheet of paper.

Match the equipment cards to the Zones and arrange them on the graph sheet. When moving equipment around on the graph sheet, four things need to be remembered:

There is a top and a bottom to each drawing on the cards provided. Keep the direction of all your equipment standard. Always keep the edges of your equipment

cards aligned to the grid.
You can turn the equipment cards over, to reverse their direction.
If you want to decrease the distance between pieces of equipment, feel free to overlap the cards.

Once you have an arrangement that you feel is satisfactory, use the Guidelines Checklist provided to evaluate your layout scheme.

If you are satisfied that your arrangement meets the checklist requirements, place a sheet of tracing paper over the graph sheet and cards, tape it down, then trace the site plus equipment.

You should try several different zone and equipment arrangements, following the same procedure each time, until you have several tracings to compare. Then, select the best alternative from the set.

Guidelines Checklist

If there are swings, allow space for moving in front and behind, without children getting hit.

If there are good, sturdy trees and suitable grassy hills, try to include them in your design plan as play places.

If there are tall structures, use soft surfaces underneath in the event of falls.

Be sure to include places for litter and for small toy storage, and for storing wheeled

toys. It is better to have several small closely spaced play areas than one or two large zones.

If you have riding toys, such as trikes or wagons, leave an open, smooth surface where it will not interfere with other activities. The same is true for ball playing -- leave enough room for bouncing, throwing and rolling, away from windows, streets, or places where the ball may interfere with other children playing.

If you need garden space, put it in a well protected area. Planted trees need borders for added protection.

If there are slides, make sure there are at least four feet of space around the base, for waiting-a-turn or just running.

Younger children should have separate play areas for safety, but they do not need to be isolated from older children's play areas.

If children of different ages and sizes will be using the playground, make certain that you have allowed for the differences in skill levels. Each age group should have a place where they feel comfortable and can play safely.

The most popular playgrounds have variety and are located in pleasant areas. Children prefer playgrounds that have familiar types of equipment (swings, slides, jungle gyms); but it is also good to have a space for adventure play, where they can build their own structures out of tires and light weight boards.

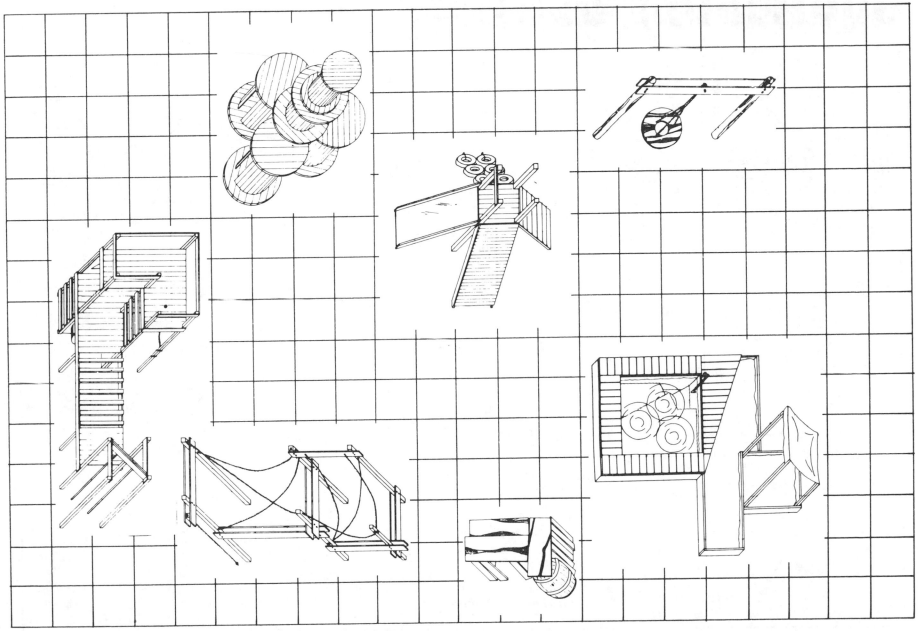

Illustration of a playground plan using equipment settings.

equipment settings

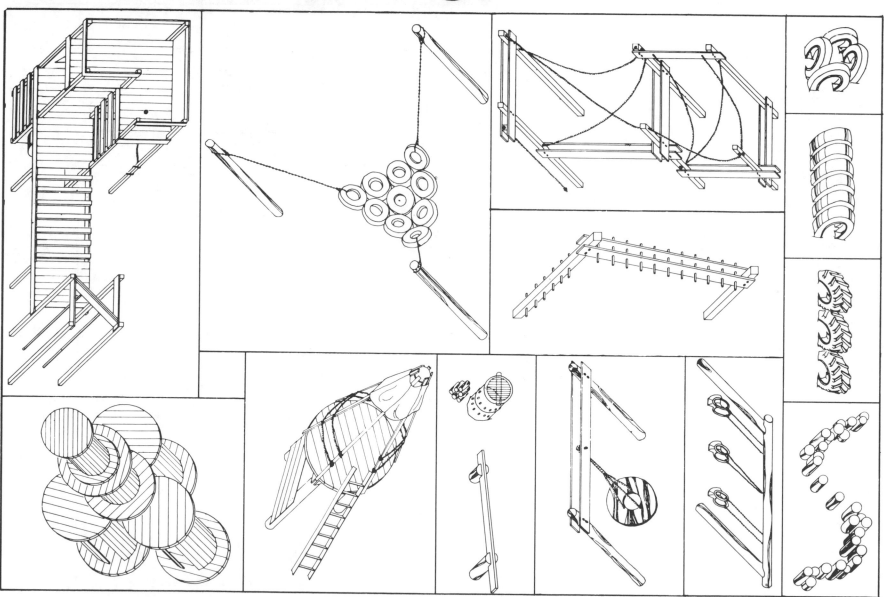

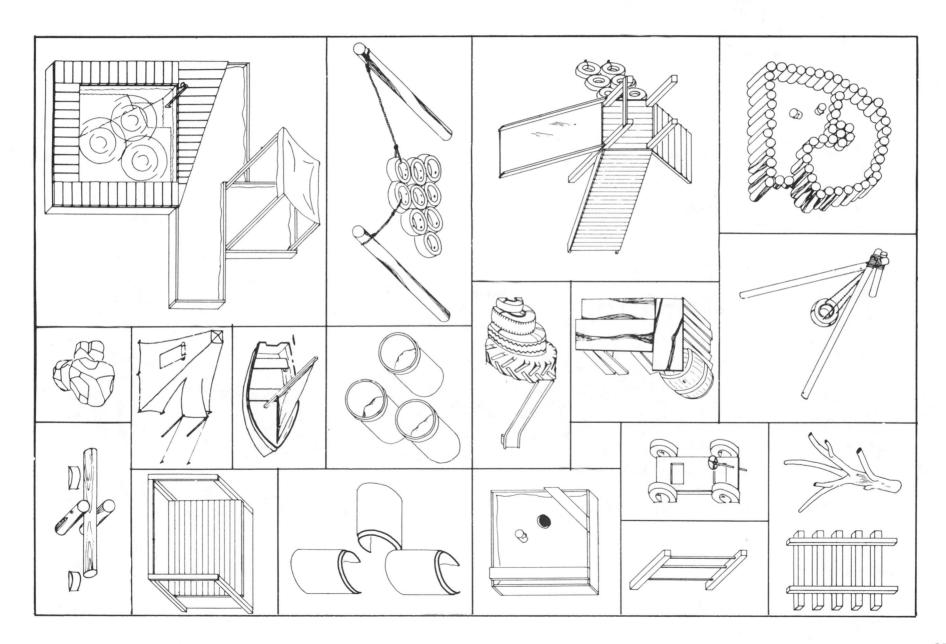

references

Almy, M., Chittenden, E., and Miller, P. *Young Children's Thinking.* New York: Columbia University Press, 1967.

Association for Childhood Education International. *Housing for Early Childhood Education.* Washington: ACEI, 1967

Bereiter, C. and Englemann, S. *Teaching Disadvantaged Children in the Pre-School.* New Jersey: Prentice Hall Inc., 1966.

Beckwith, J. *Build Your Own Playground.* Boston: Houghton Mifflin Inc., 1974.

Bengtsson, A. *Adventure Playgrounds.* New York: Praeger Publishers Inc., 1972.

Biber, B., Shapiro, E., and Wickens, D. *Promoting Cognitive Growth.* New York: Bank Street College of Education, 1971.

Blackie, J. *Inside the Primary School.* London: Her Majesty's Stationery Office, 1967.

Borton, T. *Reach, Touch and Teach.* New York: McGraw Hill Book Co., 1970.

Brearly, M., and Hitchfield, E. *A Guide to Reading Piaget.* New York: Schoken Books, 1970.

Brearley, M., editor. *The Teaching of Young Children.* New York: Schoken Books, 1970.

Bremer, J., and von Moschzisker, M. *The School Without Walls.* New York: Holt, Rinehart and Winston, Inc., 1971.

Bruner, J., *Toward a Theory of Instruction.* Cambridge, Mass: Harvard University Press, 1966.

Bruner, J. *The Process of Education.* Cambridge, Mass: Harvard University Press, 1966.

Chukousky, K. *From Two to Five.* Berkeley, Calif.: University of California Press, 1971.

Central Mortgage and Housing Corp. *Creative Playground Information Kit 1.* Ottawa: Central Mortgage and Housing Corp., 1976.

Dattner, R. *Design for Play.* New York: Van Nostrand Reinhold, 1969.

Dennison, G. *The Lives of Children.* New York: Random House, 1969.

Department of Education and Science. *Evelyn Lowe Primary School, London.* London: Building Bulletin No. 36, Her Majesty's Stationery Office, 1967.

Deutsch, M. *The Disadvantaged Child.* New York: Basic Books Inc., 1967.

Edelson, K., and Orem, R., editors. *Children's House, Parent/Teacher Guide to Montessori.* New York: Capricorn Books, 1970.

Evans, E., Shub, B., and Weinstein, M. *Day Care: How to Plan, Develop and Operate a Day Care Center.* Boston: Beacon Press, 1971.

Farallones Institute. *Farallones Scrapbook.* New York: Random House, 1971.

Fraiberg, S. *The Majic Years.* New York: Charles Scribner and Sons, 1959.

Friedberg, P. *Handcrafted Playgrounds.* New York: Vintage Books, 1975.

Frost, J., editor. *Early Childhood Education Rediscovered.* New York: Holt, Rinehart and Winston, 1968.

Gardner, D., and Cass, J. *The Role of the Teacher in the Infant and Nursery School.* New York: Pergamon Press, 1965.

Goodman, P. *Compulsory Mis- Education.* New York: Horizon Press, 1964.

The Great Atlantic and Pacific School Conspiracy. *Doing Your Own School.* Boston: Beacon Press, 1972.

Gump, P. "Environmental Psychology and the Behavior Setting," in *Responding to Social Change,* edited by B. Honikman, Stroudsburg: Dowden, Hutchinson and Ross, Inc., 1975.

Haase, R. *Designing the Child Development Center.* Washington: Project Head-Start, Dept. of Health, Education and Welfare, 1968.

Hainstock, E. *Teaching Montessori in the Home: The Pre-School Years.* New York: Random House, 1968.

Hartley, R. and others. *Understanding Children's Play.* New York: Columbia University Press, 1956.

Hentoff, N. *Our Children are Dying.* New York: Viking Press, 1966.

Hertzberg, A., and Stone, E. *Schools are for Children.* New York: Schocken Books, 1971.

Holt, J. *How Children Fail.* New York: Dell Publishing Co., 1971.

Holt, J. *How Children Learn.* New York: Dell Publishing Co., 1971.

Holt, J. *What Do I Do Monday?* New York: Dell Publishing Co., 1970.

Hymes, J. *Teaching the Child Under Six.* Columbus: Charles E. Merrill Publishing Co., 1968.

Illich, I. *Deschooling Society.* New York: Harper and Row, 1970.

Isaacs, S. *The Nursery Years.* New York: Schocken Books, 1968.

Keister, M. *The Good Life for Infants and Toddlers.* Washington: National Association for the Education of Young Children, 1971.

Koch, K. *Wishes, Lies and Dreams.* New York: Vintage Books, 1971.

Kohl, H. *The Open Classroom.* New York: Vintage Books, 1969.

Kozol, J. *Free Schools.* Boston: Houghton Mifflin Co., 1972.

Kritchevsky, S., Prescott, E., and Walling, L. "Planning Environments for Young Children," in *Alternative Learning Environments,* edited by G. Coates. Stroudsburg: Dowden, Hutchinson and Ross, Inc., 1974.

Leonard, G. *Education and Ecstasy.* New York: Delacorte Press, 1968.

Maccoby, E., and Zellner, M. *Experiments in Primary Education: Aspects of Project Follow Through.* New York: Harcourt, Brace and Jovanovich, Inc., 1970.

Marshall, S. *Adventure in Creative Education.* New York: Pergamon Press, 1967.

Marshall, S. *An Experiment in Education.* New York: Cambridge University Press, 1968.

Matterson, E. *Play and Playthings for the Preschool Child.* Baltimore: Penguine Books, 1967.

Neill, A. *Summerhill.* New York: Hart Publishing Co., 1960.

Nimnicht, G., McAfee, O., and Meier, J. *The New Nursery School.* New York: General Learning Corp., 1969.

Osman, F. *Patterns for Designing Children's Centers.* New York: Educational Facilities Laboratory, 1971.

Piaget, J., and Inhelder, B. *The Psychology of the Child.* New York: Basic Books, 1969.

Piaget, J. *Science of Education and the Psychology of the Child.* New York: Viking Press, 1971.

Pitcher, E., Lasher, M., Feinburg, S., and Hammond, N. *Helping Young Children Learn.* Columbus: Charles E. Merrill Publishing Co., 1966.

Pollowy, A. *The Urban Nest.* Stroudsburg: Dowden, Hutchinson and Ross, Inc., 1977.

Postman, N., and Weingartner, C. *The School Book.* New York: Delacorte Press, 1973.

Rathbone, C., editor. *Open Education.* New York: Citation Press, 1971.

Repo, S., editor. *This Book is About Schools.* New York: Vintage Books, 1970.

Rogers, C. *Freedom to Learn.* Columbus: Charles E. Merrill Publishing Co., 1969.

Rogers, V. *Teaching in the British Primary School.* New York: MacMillan, 1970.

Sanoff, H. *Designing With Community Participation.* New York: McGraw Hill, 1978.

Sharkey, T. *Cardboard Carpentry Workshop.* Newton, Mass: Educational Development Center, 1968.

Sharp, E. *Thinking is Child's Play.* New York: Discus/ Avon Books, 1969.

Silberman, C. *Crisis in the Classroom.* New York: Random House, 1970.

Skutch, M. and Hamlin, W. *To Start a School.* Boston: Little Brown and Co., 1971.

Warner, S. *Teacher.* New York: Simon and Schuster Inc., 1963.

Washington Environmental Yard. *Project Brochure.* Berkeley: Washington Elementary, University Laboratory School, 1972.

Weber, L. *The English Infant School and Informal Education.* New Jersey: Prentice Hall Inc., 1971.

Weikart, D., Rogers, L., Adcock, C., and McClelland, D. *The Cognitively Oriented Curriculum.* Washington: National Assoc. for the Education of Young Children, 1971.